JUNE 96

Press Pause on Your Life

Press Pause
on Your Life

ROY SHEPPARD

Thorsons
An Imprint of HarperCollins*Publishers*

Thorsons
An Imprint of HarperCollins*Publishers*
77–85 Fulham Palace Road,
Hammersmith, London W6 8JB

Published by Thorsons 1993
10 9 8 7 6 5 4 3 2 1

Roy Sheppard asserts the moral right to
be identified as the author of this work

A catalogue record for this book
is available from the British Library

ISBN 0 7225 2848 5

Phototypeset by Harper Phototypesetters Limited,
Northampton, England
Printed in Great Britain by
HarperCollinsManufacturing Glasgow

Contents

Acknowledgements

I would like to take this opportunity to thank many of my friends and colleagues for their invaluable contributions while I was preparing this manuscript. In particular I am indebted to the following people:

Ian Windsor, Simon Veale, Kate Bevan, Frankie Blagden and Deborah Schooley.

Adrian Ramskill of Coutts Career Consultants Ltd. for his kind permission to use some of the training material we originally prepared together.

Malcolm Levense of London for supplying the clothes for the front cover photograph.

My brother Glyn for giving me permission to tell the very personal story of how he nearly died climbing Annapurna 4 in the Himalayas.

I would also like to thank those colleagues in radio, television, advertising and public relations for their help and suggestions for the text. I respect their requests for anonymity.

Finally, I am indebted to hundreds of my radio and television interviewees for the time they gave up in their very busy schedules to allow me to question them about their successes, failures and aspirations.

Thank you all.

Introduction

Some time ago I came to realize that even though I led a busy and relatively successful life, I was not in control. I started to think how marvellous it would be if I could 'press pause' on my life and take the time to try and make sense of all the confusion, to identify what was distracting me from my goals and ambitions. This book is the result of what has turned out to be a considerable amount of research. I set out believing my own mind: during the past six months I have had to question even that!

I have found that many of the existing 'success' books are written using a tried and tested format. All too often they contain page after page of unattributed and unsubstantiated stories conveniently illustrating the author's 'uplifting' messages. No doubt these books have proved invaluable to millions of people, but I couldn't help thinking that there was something missing.

In the light of my research I firmly believe that this book is different. So many self-improvement books promise instant riches, immediate success, fulfilment and happiness. This one does not. This book tries only to provide you with the necessary food for thought to help you re-evaluate what you feel about being a 'success'. You will discover a different approach to success; one that is more in tune with the complex and sophisticated society we now live in.

These days people tend to get bogged down with the relatively insignificant matters in their lives, leaving little or no time to devote to the activities that *really* matter to them. This book will provide you with a better understanding of why you have not been as successful as you might have hoped. I am convinced that this information, and the insights it will provide you with, will make your future dreams of success far more attainable.

As a radio and television journalist and anchorman I have devoted a great deal of time to interviewing the rich and famous. My radio programme *Success with Roy Sheppard* on LBC in London focused specifically on discovering what it takes to be a 'success'. The audience was able to hear what made a successful person 'tick' and how the reality of his or her success is often very different to what the public is generally led to believe.

My guests have included businesspeople such as Sir Peter Parker (the former Chairman of British Rail) and Debbie Moore (of the leisure company Pineapple), mountaineer Chris Bonington, Nobel Prize-winning scientist Dr Carl Djerrassi (widely regarded as the 'father' of the birth control pill), Edward de Bono (the writer and psychologist who has given us 'lateral thinking'), the British Olympic gold medalist David Hemery, internationally-acclaimed opera singer Lesley Garrett, *War of the Worlds* musician Jeff Wayne, actor Charles Dance, best-selling author and politician Jeffrey Archer, and Tania Aebie, the youngest woman to sail solo around the globe.

It may seem unfair to highlight one particular guest as they have all been remarkable, but I will never forget the afternoon I spent with the wildlife painter and environmentalist David Shepherd at his home and studio in the Surrey countryside. I have never met anyone who is so full of joy for what he does. He gave off such contagious enthusiasm as he showed me around his private art collection and his works in progress, which at that time included a massive painting that was about to be auctioned to raise money to help protect the African elephant. David feels genuinely indebted to these elephants for providing him, through his paintings, with such a fulfilling and financially rewarding career. I remember thinking how marvellous it would be if we could all share his huge appetite for life and living.

Rarely did any of the people I've spoken with achieve 'overnight' success. It was nearly always the result of years of dedication, devotion and effort in their chosen field. Many endured enormous hardship, disappointment and setbacks with little or no guarantee of future achievement. But they proved, through dogged determination and a belief in what they did, that it was all worth while.

The record producer Mickie Most (a millionaire by the age of 24) spoke for many of those I've interviewed when he told me that in his opinion the single most important reason why most people do *not* become successful is they concentrate too much on trying to make money instead of doing something they care about. He went on to say that if those people devoted as much time and effort to doing something they enjoyed, the money would take care of itself. Obviously luck often plays its part, but ultimately success is largely down to a person's devotion to a particular 'passion' in life. Success does not have to mean financial reward. Of course, even Mickie Most agreed that it helps if you get involved in something where there is the opportunity to derive a healthy financial return!

So there it is – the simple secret for future success: passion. Or is it so simple?

All the successful people I have met have a high level of control in their lives. This control has not come about simply as a result of their success, it has invariably been a part of their lives before they 'made it'. Such 'control' enables successful people to keep their eyes on what they want to achieve.

Do you have as much control as you would like? Or do you feel that, at times, life's pressures become so great everything seems to be hurtling out of control?

You cannot be successful if you are not in control of your life. And you cannot be in control unless you are fully aware of what is going on in your life.

Press pause on *your* life as you read the chapters that follow.

Apply what you'll find in this book to your own unique circumstances so that you'll be able to devote much more time and energy towards achieving your goals (goal-setting is dealt with in detail in Chapter 8). Once you learn to see that your personal priorities are achievable, you too will be assured of the opportunity to lead a happier, more relaxed and rewarding life. This book is unashamedly biased in your favour, although it has been written with a journalistic approach to the subject.

You might find it useful, for future reference, to highlight the sentences or passages in this book that are of particular relevance to you. You will then be able to reacquaint yourself with all the points you found useful the first time around. Might I also suggest that you make a note to reread this book in about six months' time?

1

Are You in Control?

Who Is Running Your Life?

Going through life is very much like driving an automobile. You have many choices: you can take the driver's seat or be a passenger, decide where you want to go, work out how to get there, prepare for the trip and then purposefully set off towards your chosen destination. Your training will enable you to manoeuvre the vehicle around bends and to avoid potholes, pedestrians and problems. By being relatively 'in control' you will be better equipped to cope with the unforeseen. Eventually it is more than likely that you will reach your destination.

Alternatively, you can just hop on board with little or no knowledge of how to drive, start up without checking the vehicle's road-worthiness and set off with nothing more than enthusiasm in whichever direction takes your fancy. You might take a few corners too fast, spin off once or twice, get a couple of punctures, dent the bodywork, ruin the paintwork and suspension, or even break down lost in the middle of nowhere.

This second option may sound exciting and adventurous but the trouble is in reality such trips are not that enjoyable. They cause a great deal of unnecessary stress, pain and anxiety. Invariably you don't get to where you want to go (if, indeed, you knew in the first place) and such trips are so exhausting and demanding you won't even have the time to enjoy them.

Living life in this way, leaving your future in the hands of 'fate' or waiting to 'see what happens' has much romance attached to it. But in today's highly computerized society it has become possible for the first time in history to construct an environment in which highly professional corporations, governments and even individuals can make all sorts of things 'happen' to you. Your life is deliberately filled with 'distractions' of every type. Some may last for hours each day (such as watching television), while others last for just a few seconds (reading strategically placed posters and hoardings). No one forces you to do these things; some of the time we are not even aware of our behaviour.

In extreme cases, some individuals unwittingly allow themselves to be distracted to such an extent that they never have time to think about what they want to achieve in life. They will live their entire life accepting or reacting to whatever is placed in front of them day after day, year after year.

Many examples of uninvited intrusions into our lives will be given in the following chapters. You will also see how we have been conditioned to accept such widespread distraction.

Society now operates at such a highly professional level that any individual who goes through life unaware of what is being made to happen to them on a daily basis will almost certainly fail to achieve as much as they could. As ridiculous as it might at first sound, never before has there been such a need for a *professional* approach to life! Living your life 'on purpose' is only possible if you possess the capacity to exert a high degree of control over your actions. For example, professional sports and business people have far more skill and control over their actions than any amateur, however enthusiastic or talented they may be.

Control is what makes the difference between success and failure. It's the difference between *letting* things happen and *making* things happen.

I have recently returned from a filming trip to a prestigious golf club in Spain. While there I was Master of Ceremonies at a gala dinner where I sat next to the key speaker, the golfer Tony

Jacklin, a former British Open champion and winning Ryder Cup captain.

During the meal we talked about control and how he deals with the stresses of playing in front of large crowds when the stakes are high. He told me that it is essential to keep your mind in the present. If he finds that his mind is jumping ahead in time, he actually tells his brain to 'mind its own business' about the future. This has the effect of calming his nerves and minimizing distracting and damaging thoughts.

The prizes in life go to those who can exert control over their thoughts and actions when they need to. Look at the people you know – how many of them go through life constantly 'fire-fighting': attending only to the most urgent deadlines as they occur? Chances are you know a lot of people like this.

Control is often only thought of in its restrictive sense: saying 'no' to temptation and such like. But controlling your life is about purpose: understanding what you want to achieve and knowing how to go about getting it.

If *you* are not in control – you are controlled by *others*. To go back to the automobile analogy, as you drive along in life you will be subjected to countless interruptions – from family, friends, employers, employees or clients. Some are welcome, others are not. People in charge of their lives will be able to deal with these interruptions without it affecting their driving too much. They may end up going over some bumpy roads, but ultimately they will regain control.

On the other hand, individuals who are not in charge of their lives tend to accept the fact that others will grab hold of the steering wheel or even force them out of the driver's seat for a while. The results can be catastrophic.

We are all subject to unexpected tugs at the wheel from a multitude of outside forces. These forces are extremely powerful and influence us in all manner of ways. It is often difficult or even impossible to know when these forces are being exerted on your 'steering wheel'. Over a long period of time, they can take you well off course.

Often without even realizing it we are influenced to a greater or lesser degree by these outside forces. The more 'civilized' our society becomes, the more sophisticated are its persuasion tactics. By being skilfully manipulated into behaving in certain ways, our time and energies are diluted and diverted towards activities that derive many benefits for the 'persuaders': profit, political power and social influence – and precious few for ourselves.

By learning to recognize and understand these forces it is possible to overcome them.

In very simple terms the difference between a 'success' and someone who isn't is whether he spends the majority of his time and energy doing what he chooses to do or spends it doing what 'must' be done. Of course it is not always practical or desirable to avoid certain family or work-related commitments, but the more you allow others to 'steal' your time, the less control you have. I would also add that if others know that they can get away with it, they will steal more and more of your life.

My research has certainly helped me to identify the numerous occasions when others are trying to pull my strings. Interestingly, now that I'm aware of what I am subjected to I feel quite powerful: I'm in on the secret that so many others remain unaware of. This in itself has given me more self-confidence.

Increased personal control is not only possible, it is your right. The knowledge that I am now in far more control of my own thoughts has made a huge difference to the way I look at my life. I want it to do the same for you.

2

I Can't Get No Satisfaction: Maslow's 'Grumble Theory'

On the face of it we are luckier than previous generations to live in a society with far less disease, starvation and poverty. We rarely have to go without the necessities of life. Our homes are equipped with efficient sanitation, heating, lighting, the latest labour-saving gadgets and electronic consumer toys such as televisions, music systems and electronic video games, personal computers and all manner of other devices equipped with microchips, processors and electric motors. Our shops and showrooms are full of products designed to make our lives easier and more enjoyable. In the words of the former British prime minister Harold MacMillan, 'We have never had it so good.'

Surely then, we must be living in a utopian society? I don't think you would find too many people who would say – or feel – that this is true.

As I travel almost daily on the train and underground to recording studios in London, I've probably seen tens of thousands of people, all of whom look the same: downright miserable. Their faces wear blank, tired expressions. In the mornings they look half-asleep, in the evenings only half-awake. I am sure that many of them are prone to saying to themselves 'Is this *it*? Is *this* what life is all about?'

Our society seems to offer so much, why do we still want a little bit more? The eminent American psychologist Abraham H. Maslow is famous for his theory of 'the hierarchy of needs' (more of which later); he is also responsible for another theory which relates directly to this widespread dissatisfaction: the 'Grumble Theory'.

The Grumble Theory states that satisfaction of our needs leads only to temporary happiness which tends to be followed by the desire for more and ever higher levels of gratification. An upward spiral is created whereby our threshold of happiness is raised each time we experience a higher level of success or fulfilment. The result is that we are *never* happy with what we have; we imagine that just a little more will make all the difference.

Research has confirmed Maslow's theory. In a particular study it was discovered that when asked 'How much money would you need to be happy?' those questioned tended to think that an extra 25 per cent of their present income would make them happy. The trouble is – we *always* want about 25 per cent more, of everything, regardless of how much money, time or power we already have. This idea of wanting 25 per cent more is actively encouraged in our consumer society; we are constantly being persuaded to aspire for 'the best that money can buy'.

Among the rich and famous you will find many who are unfulfilled and dissatisfied – could it be that they, too, still want an extra 25 per cent? This might partially explain the widespread drug and alcohol abuse among these people, especially in showbusiness, but also, increasingly in commerce. Think of the pop and movie stars who wanted 'more' but in their pursuit of the higher 'high' paid the ultimate price: Marilyn Monroe, Janis Joplin, John Belushi, Jimi Hendrix, Jim Morrison and Tony Hancock are names that spring to mind – there are many more. The actual cause of death of each may have differed slightly but they all died well before their time.

I am certainly no movie star – but I have faced a full auditorium from a West End stage and 'performed' on live network television on a daily basis for many years, so I have a pretty good idea of what it is like to feel the rush of pure adrenalin to my system. It is difficult to describe – for some performers it is instantly addictive. Mixed with fame and mass adoration, they crave it for the rest of their lives. There are a large group of 'celebrity-junkies' who, as was said by the socialite 'Bubbles' Rothermere, will attend 'the opening of an envelope' if it means they will get in the papers or on television! To derive a similar or more intense feeling without using illegal substances might be regarded by some as an impossibility. (This is not intended to condone such behaviour, but I think it goes some way towards trying to explain it.)

To a much lesser degree, the rest of us also suffer from the detrimental side-effects of success: each time we experience a new 'high' our own threshold of excitement rises – we need more next time to be similarly happy. The overall effect is one of becoming permanently 'happily discontented' with what life has to offer.

The fact that self-improvement books sell in their millions is proof that a huge number of people are dissatisfied with their position in life. They want more money, happiness, satisfaction, respect, love and power. The majority of such books strengthen the idea that the more we achieve and the more we surround ourselves with the accoutrements of successful living, the happier we will become and the more successful we will be.

Our personal feelings of unfulfilment and dissatisfaction stem from this pressure to increase continuously our income and our buying power. Once we achieve an extra 25 per cent in our life, there are always more pressures exerted on our time and wallet to force us into striving for 'just a little bit more'. The end result is invariably physical and mental exhaustion, stress and more dissatisfaction. We never have enough time to enjoy and savour what we have.

Commercialism, if not fully to blame, must accept a large part of the responsibility for conditioning us into wanting more. We are continually sold the promise of future success and happiness if we buy more and more products. It is a hollow promise. In the eyes of commerce, we can *never* be active enough in our buying. All manufacturers and retailers want us to increase our consumption every month and every year. Throughout the world, governments and corporations are constantly striving for economic growth. The only way this can be achieved is through increased consumption. This simply cannot continue for ever.

We are manipulated and controlled on a massive scale to ensure that the status quo is maintained. Anyone publicly denouncing the '25 per cent extra' system risks ridicule, often by those with the commercial interests to perpetuate the myth that our lives will be enriched if we consume products made or sold by them.

Maslow's 'hierarchy of needs' states that we all have certain basic needs that we seek instinctively to gratify: self-preservation of life, protection, food, shelter, respect, knowledge, aesthetic appreciation, love, sex and a need for self-fulfilment.

So, what happens now that we live in a society where most of these needs are already satisfied? The answer is that new ones are created specially for us. The science of what motivates us to satisfy our needs is so thoroughly researched and widely distributed to governments and industry that we can now be controlled and manipulated on a scale previously unimaginable. As we can only make decisions based on the information we are given, any organization seeking to control and influence us has only to control the information supplied to us.

It is quite paradoxical that in 'free' and 'democratic' societies public opinion, behaviour and buying patterns can be so carefully and successfully orchestrated. The great thing for these professional manipulators is that we, the public, believe that we are making up our own minds! Could it be that George Orwell's 'Big Brother' does exist, but he has learned subtlety, friendliness and the art of smiling benignly?

Discussing the content of this book with friends and colleagues has occasionally evoked the response 'Roy, you're being anti-capitalist and trying to fight consumerism.' This book isn't about 'fighting' anything, certainly not the capitalist system! It is only concerned with providing you with an awareness of the forces in our society which can, if allowed to dominate life, result in unhappiness, frustration and a lack of control. My point is: just because an individual is asked, persuaded or manipulated into accepting whatever he or she is offered, this does not, by definition, mean that it is worth having.

To be in control we need to be able to slow down, to stand back from our complex living and working environments so that we can see more clearly what is going on, what we are being subjected to, what we are doing and – most importantly – why? Being aware of all these things will go a long way towards helping you to change and improve your future.

So, *slow down. Press pause on your life.* Learn to say *no.*

The pace of life in our sophisticated society is now faster than it has *ever* been, so much so that it has become an achievement in itself just to be able to cope with it. We are forced into juggling responsibilities, deadlines and finances. There is never enough time or enough money to go around. It is small wonder so few people achieve what they consider to be their full potential. How can they if most of their effort is devoted towards merely trying to cope with whatever life throws at them?

We have been brainwashed into feeling the need to consume more and more. We are positively encouraged to do so again and again. Technology and production techniques are now so advanced that production often outstrips genuine demand. The only way for manufacturers to solve this problem is to stimulate demand by persuading us that buying more will make us feel better. The overall effect of this over-consumption has not only created a population that feels there is something 'lacking' in their life, it is also devastating the environment: we have consumed more in the last hundred years than in any similar period in the history of the world. Nor is there any sign of it decreasing. We have been fed the idea that we can consume ourselves to happiness. The sooner we learn that this is hogwash, the more chance each one of us will have of becoming genuinely happier.

A higher rate of consumption does not mean a higher quality of life. This is a sobering thought: 5 per cent of the world's population consume ⅓ of the world's natural resources. Needless to say – we are that 5 per cent!

Manufacturers will stop at nothing to persuade you to buy – they don't actually care whether you need what they have to sell, all they say is 'Buy, buy, buy!' Every reputable company is now heavily committed to improving quality throughout their organizations; in their products, customer service, administration, planning, design and marketing. Their customers will undoubtedly benefit, but sadly the motivating force is less altruistic – forward thinking companies realize that competition is likely to become so intense in the next decade that they must make these improvements if they are to survive and prosper.

For a large number of people, shopping has become a substitute for feelings of personal well-being – it is said that 59 per cent of Americans are actually addicted to shopping, and I have even heard the argument that consuming more is actually the patriotic thing to do! It is said that our economy relies on increased consumption – if we don't keep buying we will put more people out of work, factories will close and our country will become weaker in the world economy. What a load of baloney.

Advertising is geared towards encouraging higher consumption, discarding products before they are worn out to buy newer more 'up to date' replacements. Effective image building has successfully made it unfashionable to repair broken items and appliances. We are made to feel that the only people who go to the trouble to repair things are those who cannot afford to buy new products; the implication being that if you cannot afford something, you must be a failure. Repairing items is often made as difficult as possible by manufacturers who deliberately engineer the following response from us: 'It's not worth repairing; I may as well buy a replacement'. The cost of spare parts is often intentionally high to coax you into making your 'buy new' decision.

Funnily enough, as I was writing this my old personal computer finally died and went to PC heaven. No matter how hard I tried I could not find anyone to repair it. I eventually managed to contact the manufacturer. Their spokesperson said 'We don't make those any more – we don't even have replacement parts for them – can I recommend that you buy a new machine?' He then went into a sales pitch about their latest models, but would not be drawn on my questions about how long *they* have been designed to survive before I wouldn't be able to get replacement parts! By sheer luck, a friend had an identical computer, which he had hardly ever used, and he offered it to me!

I am not an environmental missionary; it just makes sense to reduce consumption. This does not mean that you must sell your car, buy a bicycle and stop buying anything else! By learning to consume *less* of everything, from food to all consumer goods, you will actually reduce your personal levels of stress, improve your future sense of well-being and help to prolong the life of this planet of ours.

3

What Are You Up Against?

I have a confession to make: for the past 10 years I have been a professional persuader, part of the multi-billion-pound manipulation industry in Britain. I have been paid to cajole you into buying everything from the music of Michael Jackson to orange juice, chocolates, electrical goods, automobiles and many other products and services. First as an announcer for BBC radio and television I spent a number of years devoted to the 'science' of encouraging you to watch more television and listen to more radio. Then for over three years I was an anchorman for the evening BBC television news in London.

This work has given me a unique insight into how we are constantly pushed and pulled in all directions by people and organizations who have a vested interest in influencing our behaviour. I can assure you, *you have no idea what you're up against!* The techniques used to sell products, ambitions, political ideologies and attitudes are now so sophisticated, well researched and well resourced that it has reached the stage where the manipulators know more about us than we know about ourselves. We conform to their expectations: our behaviour has become as homogenized as many of the products we buy.

The manipulation industry resembles a giant iceberg: you see only the tip; there is *far* more going on beneath the surface. Many of those who work in persuasion-related businesses would prefer it if you couldn't see the iceberg at all. The persuaders themselves have little to worry about: their future is not only secure, it is looking quite bright. Personal disposable income in the United States alone is an astounding $3,946,100 million (1990), while here in Britain it was £298,136 million (1991).[1] With this much money burning a hole in our pockets you can bet a lot of effort goes into convincing us to hand it over.

It is not entirely fair to say that corporations don't care whether the products they produce are genuinely needed or are unnecessarily wasteful of raw materials and damaging to the environment. The issue is far more complex and few products are produced without input from consumers. Consumer 'panels' are encouraged to assess a product's colour, style, content, environmental associations and more. Such panels effectively help companies to improve their aim when targeting prospective purchasers.

Before we look at the manipulation industry in more detail let us first turn our attention to the most popular and successful persuasion tactics used at the grassroots level: in our stores. Try to keep the following list in mind next time you shop – I guarantee you will save yourself money *and* derive a great deal of quiet satisfaction that you are not being duped or 'operated on'.

Much of the success of the persuasion business is based on a highly developed understanding of our behaviour and habits. They rely on us to be (and we usually are):

- too busy to think or care too much about what they get up to.
- largely unaware of their activities.
- inherently greedy.
- basically lazy.
- operating under the mistaken belief that we make our own decisions and that we are logical and rational.
- behaving illogically and irrationally!

- in need of constant oral gratification.
- impulsive.
- possessed of short memories.
- docile in our attitude towards commercials.
- impatient and needing immediate satisfaction.

Armed with this knowledge (and a lot more besides) they are capable not only of fleecing us of our hard-earned cash but of systematically 'de-individualizing' us as they persuade us to buy more than we need. Each time it happens it may seem inconsequential and of little importance (and on their behalf let me thank you for such an attitude – because that is exactly what they want!), but multiplied over the course of many years the amount of control exerted over us is so great that we wind up handing over a great deal of money, much of which we had little conscious intention of spending.

If you are prone to returning from a shopping trip with far more than you intended you have probably succumbed to the skills of professional manipulators who have persuaded you to be impulsive. It has been estimated that a staggering 70 per cent of our buying is based on spur-of-the-moment decisions. With this amount of business at stake, of course our impulsiveness is going to be exploited and encouraged at every opportunity and in every conceivable way.

Many of our 'impulse' purchases are known as FMCGs (Fast-Moving Consumer Goods). These include many types of food such as savoury snacks and confectionery. Impulse snacks are one of the most profitable and fastest-growing areas of the FMCG market. (I will go into more detail about how we are manoeuvred into buying food in Chapter 4.)

One of the prime requirements for selling large quantities of FMCGs is that these products receive the widest distribution and promotion. Imagine how much easier it would be to avoid 'temptation' if it were not so easy to buy all these fattening FMCGs! Manufacturers and retailers know this very well. By repeatedly putting 'impulse' products under our noses we are more likely to say 'yes'. Widespread availability guarantees significant sales for producers and retailers alike.

Ask yourself why you have reached out for specific products in the past. There are a number of possible reasons: habit, an advertisement, word of mouth or, very simply, the packaging may have caught your eye. Impulse purchases rely very heavily on package design. Bright colours such as red and yellow are popular, while typeface sizes and styles are chosen meticulously. All designs are thoroughly tested before they are put into production, as research has shown that poorly-designed packaging can 'kill' a product in the marketplace. The stakes are too high to let this happen.

Notice how all manufacturers use words like *New, Improved, Free, Reduced, Extra, Natural, Environmentally Friendly, Fuller Flavour, Value, You, Exciting* and *Low-Price* to attract attention and stimulate sales. Packages are often 'flashed' or highlighted with special offers, etc. to serve as 'flag-wavers' on the shelf – effectively saying 'Hey you – come over here – have a look at me, go on, buy me, you won't be sorry. So what if you don't actually need me, don't think about that, just put me in your shopping trolley!' Often packages are designed to persuade us simply to pick them up at first: what's written on them is in deliberately small print to ensure that we cannot read it properly unless we take it off the shelf. Research has shown that once these items are in our hands, a high enough percentage of us does not put them back.

Millions of pounds and dollars are spent on *POS* (Point of Sale) material in another attempt to attract our attention; specially designed and constructed displays, expensively printed leaflets and brochures and even demonstration videos. The role of Point of Sale activity is to ensure that the consumer *has* to make a conscious decision *not* to buy the product.

We are led to believe that our impulsiveness comes from within ourselves – but this is not the case. Just look around your home. How many disused items can you find which seemed a good idea at the time you bought them? There is widespread acceptance within retailing that 'impulse' purchases are usually priced up to £29.99. However, I know someone who actually bought a brand-new car on impulse (it helped that her father owns an airline, a travel business and a couple of exclusive hotels – even so, her husband was rather surprised!). Normally anything over about £29.99 requires a different set of techniques to get us to pay out our money. I will look at these techniques in a moment.

The next time you go shopping, try to be more aware of what is happening around you. Does the piped music help you to feel more relaxed? Some of the larger supermarkets with on-site bakeries also 'pipe' baking smells back into the store. It increases bread and cake sales. The Japanese have developed synthetically produced smells which are pumped through the air-conditioning systems of a variety of stores. A London company, Marketing Aromatics, are said to supply such smells to retailers seeking to increase sales. They include 'cut grass' for fruit shops, 'leather' for car showrooms and even 'coconut' for travel agents.

Food retailing has developed into a highly sophisticated science whereby, like sheep, we are led through the shop buying as effortlessly (and unthinkingly) as they can engineer. How does the layout of the store affect your route through it? Controlling customer flow plays a key role in persuading us to buy. Store layouts are often designed by computer programmes (such as 'Spaceman') which calculate the optimum use of store space and help retailers to decide which products should be displayed in particular places. They define what are known as shop 'hot spots': areas of a store where sales are especially high. Items placed at the end of a shelf unit will attract high impulse buying – the products placed there are very carefully chosen for their high profit potential. By changing the position of particular goods within a store, retailers know they can increase their sales significantly. For instance, luxury products and those with a higher profit margin tend to be displayed at eye level, while more essential items are placed higher or lower because retailers know we are prepared to search for them – why waste prime selling space on products they know will sell? Other products, such as sauces and pickles, are positioned directly above meat and frozen products to encourage 'related' buying.

Another widespread ploy to get us to buy more than we need is the creation of 'multipacks'. For example, if you want to buy one battery usually you can't, because they are deliberately made available only in packs of two or four.

Each square foot/metre of any retail shop must produce a minimum financial return for the retailer. If a product fails to attract that income it is either dropped or moved elsewhere. Many products on display are those we do not necessarily want but – attractively packaged – they will probably go into our trolleys. (By the way, even the size of the trolley is carefully calculated to hold more food than we probably were planning to buy. We wouldn't buy impulse products so readily if they did not fit easily alongside our 'essentials' in the trolley. Shopping baskets, by contrast, are often kept in deliberately out-of-the-way places to promote more trolley use.)

In addition to all of this, the sales promotion industry sets itself the task of manipulating us into speeding up the buying process, further increasing our consumption and our loyalty to specific brands. To accomplish this they use a wide variety of techniques: two-for-the-price-of-one, 'free' offers (vouchers either on the pack or to be posted for a refund) and money-off coupons for future purchases. (These rely on a redemption rate of up to 14 per cent.[2] They don't want too many people to claim, as this would cost them a lot of money!) Competitions are favoured ways of attracting our attention and distracting us from thinking about whether we actually need the product.

Much of the time the money and effort devoted towards persuading us to buy are aimed at getting us to choose one brand rather than another. But the effect of all this coercion is to create a population that suffers from 'manipulation overload'. Its more common name? *Stress.*

To get us to buy higher-priced goods, manufacturers ·and retailers rely on personal 'help' from salespeople. Professional salespeople are taught to stress the 'feel-good' factor: to make you feel good about yourself and the prospect of buying a product. This is particularly important in the clothing industry.

The best salespeople are those who have perfected the illusion that they are *not* trying to sell. They are skilful at planting images of happiness and enjoyment in the minds of their customers before they make the sale. They encourage us to 'spoil ourselves'.

Notice the following: a good salesperson will concentrate on selling the 'benefits' of a product or service rather than its features. They don't want to waste valuable selling time, so you can work out the features yourself with the instruction booklet when you get home! Watch out when you are handed a product directly – clever salespeople know that most of us instinctively accept anything we are given. Once it is in your hands they are closer to a sale.

Another favoured ploy used by sales staff is to offer a 'choice' of products. This technique fools us into forgetting our third option – saying 'no'. Most salespeople have learned through experience that most people do not really know what they want (could that mean they don't *really want or need* what they are looking at?), so when a salesperson asks what price range you are looking at he or she will almost certainly be able to 'sell up', i.e. persuade you to spend 15–20 per cent more than you intended. This happens with everything from electrical goods and vehicles to houses.

While you are being 'sold' you might sometimes notice a salesperson gently touching your arm just above the elbow. This is another technique aimed at reassuring you about the sale.

When it comes to the actual sale, retailers make it as easy as possible for you to pay by credit card, interest-free credit, finance agreements, etc. Many store groups now operate their own credit cards. These induce us to stay loyal to that particular chain. These cards also save the stores a lot of money – large credit card operators such as Visa and Mastercard charge retailers anything between 4 and 6 per cent for the convenience of each transaction. In-store cards also provide retailers with invaluable customer 'databases' that are then used to mail customers with information about special offers and promotions. They also provide vast amounts of statistical information such as our buying patterns, how much we spend and when. This data is then analysed to find new ways of getting us to buy more.

When you pay by credit card or cheque many salespeople are trained to make a point of noting and then using your name in their closing conversation. You might think 'Why would they bother?' The answer is simple – you will be more likely to return to that store to be made to feel good again. Little if anything is left to chance in retailing. There's a well known retail maxim 'Retail is detail'.

Just to give you some additional food for thought on the power of salesmanship, here are a few of the ludicrous things many of us have often been persuaded to do:

- Pay a premium for the dubious health advantages of bottled fizzy water. It is carbonated merely to titillate the taste-buds.
- Pay above the odds for the 'privilege' of wearing clothes that advertise the manufacturer's name. Whenever we buy clothing these manufacturers cater to our need to be seen to be affluent, by creating 'designer' wear. Marketers have ensured that those people who cannot afford the most expensive brand names are catered for by cheaper designer brands. From now on why not refuse to wear anything featuring designer names, their motifs or logos?
- Feel unsuccessful if we do not buy a new car every year or so, even if there is nothing wrong with the one we have.

And there are so many more! We have been conditioned to accept the unacceptable.

Political Manipulation

The power of advertising and image-creation is so great and so effective that it is now used more and more by governments.

All governments need to exert an element of control over their citizens. Methods differ: Stalin, Hitler and, more recently, Saddam Hussein prefer a 'direct' approach – 'If you don't do as I say, you will be shot or gassed!', while others (i.e., democratic governments) have to resort to more subtle and hidden techniques!

For example, from the early to mid-1980s British industry practically ground to a halt when many of the unions tried to take on the government by instigating a series of widespread labour strikes. In 1980 11,964,000 working days were lost through industrial stoppages.[3] By 1985 this figure was down to 6,402,000, and by 1990 the figure was nearer 1,903,000.[4] How was this achieved? Mass manipulation. The Government skilfully manoeuvred millions of people into a position whereby they no longer 'chose' to go on strike.

How? By encouraging blue-collar workers (those thought most likely to strike) to buy their own properties instead of paying rent to local government, a more stable workforce was created. Simultaneously, the government was able to rid itself of very costly property, much of it in need of major repair.

The Government had persuaded these people to buy property by appealing to a combination of our basic human needs as outlined by psychologist Abraham Maslow in the previous chapter: providing our own privately owned 'shelter', implying that there is more 'security' in owning your own home, appealing to our inherent 'greed' by hinting that if you own your own home you will make a lot of money from it in the future (as the saying goes, 'you can never go wrong with bricks and mortar'). And finally they sold individuals on the idea that if they bought their own home, it was proof of their 'success' in life – no longer were they just lowly workers – they were 'property owners'!

The housing market enjoyed a boom, prices soared – everybody was happy – that is, until prices plummeted, leaving many of these new homeowners with houses that a) they could not sell or b) had dropped in value to a level below the amount they were mortgaged for. When mortgage interest rates rose, these helpless individuals had to work even harder to keep up payments – and therefore they were even less likely to go on strike!

Not all political manipulation is necessarily bad. No government, regardless of what it stands for, will ever please everyone, so they have to resort to a bit of subterfuge.

Once any idea such as 'needing' to own your house becomes established in the minds of a significant number of people, it takes on an air of respectability and normality. We take it for granted and are unlikely to question whether such an idea is in our own best interests. The more this happens without our knowledge, the less we are in control of our lives. We have effectively learned to let others do part of our thinking for us.

Advertising

Advertisers have gleefully taken to the task of thinking for us. The world of advertising has meticulously created hundreds of branded products, each with its own unique image and 'personality'. Think of any particular brand and you will almost certainly have specific views on it. Let's use a Volvo car as an example. What are its qualities? It is likely you will think of Volvos as the safest cars on the road. How do you actually know that? Unless you are a safety expert your thoughts and views have almost certainly been put into your mind over many years of consistent and carefully orchestrated, paid-for advertising. You have seen so many persuasion messages reinforcing the 'safety' issue that you have learned to accept it as fact. Protecting one's family is another of Maslow's basic needs. When we decide to buy a new car, safety is a major issue for a section of the buying public – for many, a Volvo has become the only car worth considering.

I am not suggesting for a moment that Volvos are *not* safe, merely that your thoughts may not really be your own. This has become so widespread that often we no longer buy actual products – we buy the image.

Advertising has become the largest growth industry of the twentieth century, achieving enormous power and enmeshing itself so thoroughly into our society that it is impossible to think that its presence will ever diminish. The industry has become so successful that it manipulates the lives of many millions of people every single day. You can no longer see the join between what is real and what has been specially created and paid for.

This is not intended as an exposé of media power and exploitation. I have left that to Vance Packard, Eric Clark and William Meyers, authors of the highly acclaimed books *The Hidden Persuaders*, *The Want Makers* and *The Image Makers* respectively. For an insight into the world of political manipulation *Persuaders of Power: The Rise of the Political Myth-makers* (based on the BBC2 television series and written by Laurence Rees) is the book for you.

Most people believe sincerely that they are immune to the effects of advertising and sales persuasion. It is convenient for the manipulators to let them think that way. In some cases we will be told how unique, free-thinking, logical, rational, independent and shrewd we are – if that is what it takes to get us to buy or accept their propositions. There is nothing new about 'people manipulation', it is well documented. And all professional persuasion has a common aim; persuading us to say 'yes'. By learning to see many of these hidden forces we can choose not to be manipulated.

Advertising and advertisers have become so powerful that their activities are now subject to certain media industry regulations in Britain and other countries; for example, radio and television scripts must be vetted and approved before they can be broadcast. However, advertisers stretch these rules to the limit, doing whatever they can, using every technique and any weakness we may have to help sell products and services. If an advertiser can get away with a particular approach, they will try it.

It would be wrong to assume that all advertising is dishonestly manipulative. A lot of it is highly artistic, creative, tasteful and provides a genuine service to the public by supplying information about much-needed products and services. But it must be remembered that advertising portrays, by definition, a biased view of its product or service. Just like manufacturers, it is of no concern to advertising agencies that the products they try to sell for their clients may be unnecessary or a waste of our natural resources.

The real power in our society belongs to those with the skills, resources and money to convince us to do what is best for them. Personal control is based on making choices. We can only make choices based on the information we are provided with. If our information source is tampered with in any way, we can be directed into thinking and behaving in (almost) any way. Regardless of how unique you think you are and how free to make choices affecting your life, you are part of the complex world of statistics and market research. Your age, sex, earnings, social grade, political views, likes, dislikes, insecurities, anxieties, what television programmes you watch, the types of food you consume, the newspapers and magazines you read, your expenditure and time devoted to practically every leisure activity, your attitudes on most subjects – all are carefully and exactingly recorded.

The research even tells what we do during our most private moments. Forgive me for being indelicate, but toilet tissue manufacturers even have data on the number of 'folders' and 'scrunchers' (as we are called) that exist. Apparently, one of these two methods uses more tissue!

Those who employ and control these manipulation businesses take all such information very seriously indeed.

All this research is studied and interpreted continuously by a wide variety of highly paid experts including statisticians, social and behavioural psychologists and sociologists as well as advertising, marketing and sales executives. These people dedicate their working lives to finding out how to open our wallets. If we have money, they will do everything they can to get us to part with it. More often than not, they succeed.

The population at large is led along almost blind to the antics of commercialism. There is a desperate need for the public to be educated about such pressures on them. But no organization will ever do it. It is against the interests of government; to spend large sums of money showing us how to spend *less* would be unspeakable, while corporations are loath to educate consumers. They are paranoid about spending money on educating the public, because there are a number of classic marketing case histories which have proved that when Corporation A paid for an education programme relating to their products, then a competing Corporation B will spend their money on persuading us to buy the actual products from them. No one wants to be Corporation A!

Manipulation on this scale and sophistication only became possible when television established itself as an integral part of modern life. At no time in the history of humanity has it been possible to speak directly to so many millions of people in their own homes, literally at the flick of a switch.

Part of the advertiser's research has shown that a consumer must see or hear a persuasion message at least six or seven times before it will successfully convince us to buy. So every product manufacturer and service provider literally bombards us with thousands and thousands of messages, each hoping to hit us enough times to have the desired effect. Interestingly, repetition of this kind provides the basis for all hypnosis. Advertising is a form of 'suggestion'; hypnosis is merely a 'heightened state of suggestibility'. There are many parallels between the two: advertising persuades millions of people to do some very silly things. And anyone who has ever seen a stage hypnotist will agree that individuals under hypnosis can be persuaded to be even sillier! All the advertiser and the hypnotist have to do is persuade us that the suggestions they provide are rational and sensible. If our subconscious minds accept such suggestions we will act upon them. It's ironic that suggestion through advertising has been allowed to flourish, while 'mass hypnosis' is highly illegal! In Eric Clark's book *The Want Makers* he writes 'Here lies the irony: the more we are bombarded by advertising, the less we notice, and yet, almost certainly, the more we are affected.'

This is how we are systematically persuaded to go to see a movie. Before a new film comes out we will probably read about the private life of one or more of its stars in glossy magazines (Hit 1). We will see posters advertising the forthcoming release (Hit 2). We will see and hear the stars talking about the movie on numerous TV and radio chat shows (Hits 3 and 4). Press advertisements in the newspapers (Hit 5) and film reviews (Hit 6). This is a much simplified version of what actually happens, but the point is that no part of this process is accidental. The aim is to place some aspect of the movie in front of us repeatedly; this repetition is important because, after a while, it may make you feel that you have *got* to see what all the fuss is about. Bingo, all that strategic marketing and PR has worked again!

Most other products and services cannot rely on our seemingly insatiable appetite for information about glamorous movie stars, so they have to make use of repeated press and media advertising to attract attention away from competitors and so keep their name in the forefront of your mind when you buy. An estimated eight out of ten new products fail despite extensive advertising; yet the rewards are so high for the products that *do* succeed that manufacturers can afford a high failure rate. In any case, why should they care: their skills and the media airtime for the commercials they create are paid for by you and me. The advertising industry in Britain is worth approximately £6,000 million. In the US the estimated figure is a staggering $41,000 million. Everything we buy contributes to footing this bill. Some manufacturers literally throw so much money at selling their products they are effectively buying their customers!

In recent years, governments, too, have increased their use of advertising dramatically. We, the public, are made to feel that we have a 'caring' government when we see commercials for the fight against AIDS, drug abuse, etc. There is a strong argument to suggest that the vast sums spent on advertising might be better employed on actual treatment, care and research – but without advertising the government would not be *seen* to be trying to do some good.

I have on my desk in front of me a number of up-to-date books listing hundred of pages of information on you, me and millions of others like us. It is readily available to businesses to help them persuade us to buy their products and services. Here is just one piece of information that caught my eye. It is based on British shopping and leisure behaviour. There will be similar data available in other countries. Which of the following categories would you put yourself in? And which would you aspire towards?

Persona Behaviourgraphics Classification[5]

1) Golf-clubs and Volvos: Husband career-orientated, materialistic
   3.7 per cent
2) The Got Set: Higher income, well-educated, interested in arts
   1.8 per cent
3) Bon Viveurs: Winers and diners, articulate conversationalists
   4.3 per cent

4) Fast Trackers: Young, middle-income, interested in active sports, leisure
   3.6 per cent

5) The High Tecs: Motivated by technology, not necessarily high earners
   6.2 per cent

6) Faith, Hope and Charity: Churchgoers and charity donators, generally with older/grown-up children, community-minded
   3.9 per cent

7) Safe, Steady and Sensible: Mostly self-employed with health and accident insurance, savings and pension plans
   3.9 per cent

8) Craftsmen and Homemakers: Little education but useful craft skills
   6.1 per cent

9) Trinkets and Treasures: Older, middle-income group, intellectual rather than physical
   4.7 per cent

10) Cultural Travellers: Often elderly, love foreign holidays/theatre/concerts
    5.0 per cent

11) Carry On Camping: Outdoor types, like camping, walking, often in industrial and white-collar work, particularly public sector
    3.8 per cent

12) Health and Humanities: Have spiritual values, interested in political/social change
    4.2 per cent

13) Wildlife Trustees: Older, better off with country pursuits, enjoy travelling
    5.5 per cent

14) Factories, Fishing and Football: Active, outdoorsy, mostly blue-collar
    4.6 per cent

15) Lager, Crisps and Videos: Sociable materialists, pleasure-seekers, poorly paid with little education
    5.3 per cent

16) Instant Chic: Lower-income young people, interested in modern styles, eager for new experiences
    4.9 per cent

17) Gardeners' Question Time: Older, suburban/rural owner/occupiers
    5.9 per cent

18) Pools, Horses and Pubs: Poorer, less educated, few material comforts
    5.4 per cent

19) Survivors: Very poor, little education or confidence
    9.1 per cent

20) Reading, Religion and Routine: Low-income elderly, 'respectable' folk, give to charity and like to read, usually in small towns
    8.1 per cent

Advertisers will tell you that advertising does not create demand. They are quick to state that if a product does not live up to expectations it will die. The reality is that if enough people can be manipulated into believing they need something they don't, healthy profits can still be made. The less necessary a product, the more it will rely on advertising for sustained sales.

Advertising has satisfied needs where they existed and created them where they have not. The effects of this 'need-creation' have been dissatisfaction and frustration on a massive scale. Millions are duped into believing they have to acquire a whole host of new products and status symbols to prove to others that they are 'successful'. We are told what is 'trendy' and what is 'out of fashion'. Many people believe they are overweight and ugly because they compare themselves with the images featured in countless glossy magazines and throughout the rest of the media. Commercial interests callously perpetuate the falsehood that we, too, can and should try to look like these 'beautiful people'. Supermodel Cindy Crawford is quoted thus: 'People tell me women get upset because they don't look like this. What they don't realize is that *I* don't look like this, either.' Many businesses have a vested interest in being seen to offer ordinary women a 'helping hand'. Most are doing nothing of the sort. They are simply using every tool at their disposal to persuade potential customers to hand over their money.

The sooner we realize it, the sooner we would find that it is OK to be our imperfect selves.

Look at the pages of any women's magazine: there between the mouthwatering recipes for decadently delicious chocolate cakes are advertisements for a vast array of other foods and page after page of information on the latest fad diet and exercise routines. The media sends these conflicting and confusing messages continually to a population already suffering from a variety of anxieties and feelings of low self-worth. No wonder we feel inadequate – there are so many professionals who make us feel that way because it is good for their business.

Because there is so much money at stake in the perfection business, models starve themselves during the days leading up to photo sessions, then make-up, lighting and photography spend hours doing everything they can to create a single image (and that is all it is – an image), which is often designed to persuade us to buy a product. Once the photographic image is created, more experts retouch and enhance it even further. It is common practice to 'improve on perfection' in this way. Even photographs of the most beautiful women and handsome men in the world are carefully and meticulously retouched; teeth are whitened, bulges vanish with help from an air brush, jaw lines are emphasized and straightened while unwanted spots and body hair are removed with judicious help from a paint brush or electronic wizardry.

No individual can compete with the advertisers' devotion to creating images of perfection. Anyone who tries will end up feeling anything from inadequate to ugly. If we feel this way, we become even more likely to believe any promises made to improve our less-than-perfect looks. Indeed, it is said that the cosmetics business no longer sell creams and powders, they sell promises; and empty ones at that. Many manufacturers make obscene profits, often charging a small fortune for creams and lotions which they often describe using pseudo-scientific terms to try to convince insecure consumers into believing that their products hold out at least 'some' hope for prolonging youthful looks. All these products are wrapped up in fancy, designer boxes and given a hefty price tag. Detailed research has proven that if you demand a high price, enough people will believe that 'it must be good if it is expensive' although a significant percentage of the price is the cost of persuading you to buy.

In Penny Chorlton's book *Cover Up: Lifting the Lid Off the Cosmetics Industry* she states 'The cosmetics industry is a secret world, a world we know only by the hype, image and impression fed to us by the glossy world of advertising.' She also quotes the late Elizabeth Arden, founder of the massive cosmetics empire, as once describing the cosmetics industry as 'the nastiest business in the world'.

The advertising of cosmetics is one good example of how our insecurities are used against us to persuade us to buy products of questionable value. The cosmetics and food industries have a stranglehold on the media: publishers and broadcasters simply cannot afford to upset these powerful and wealthy advertisers. Time and again commercial interests get in the way of any real benefits for the consumer.

During the course of my research for this book I have discovered many areas of widespread manipulation of the public – but nowhere has it been so thorough as in the food industry. It is my belief that the food industry is directly

responsible for more unhappiness than any other industry.
The next chapter explains why.

[1] Central Statistical Office
[2] *Food Attitudes Monitor*, 1990
[3] *Financial Times*
[4] *Monthly Digest of Statistics* (HMSO), July 1991
[5] CCN Systems Ltd

Food, Glorious Food

As human beings we are obsessed with putting things into our mouths. We love to lick, crunch, suck, bite, nibble, chew and swallow food. We eat when we have nothing to do, when we are feeling depressed, stressed or happy. Oh – and we eat when we are hungry!

This deep-seated need for continual oral gratification is just one aspect of our behaviour that is fully understood and meticulously researched by every food manufacturer and retailer.

Do we really need feeding so much? Of course not – they want our money! Food growers, processors, manufacturers and sellers want us to eat all they can supply. The profits are gargantuan, and as such the industry has enormous commercial, economic and political power.

Our ability to feel 'peckish' is the basis of a hugely profitable section of the food industry. The sale of biscuits (cookies), chocolate, ice cream and savoury snacks such as crisps (potato chips) account for hundreds of millions in revenues.

Supermarkets, convenience shops, burger bars, pizza parlours, restaurants and cafés, ice-cream vendors, butchers, fruit-and-veg stalls, food outlets at petrol stations, railway stations and airports, wherever there are people, someone will sell us food. We have turned into constant 'grazers', always eating on the move. It is irrelevant to the sellers that we may not 'need' such food. And why should they care that the food they sell contributes to such widespread obesity in our society? If we as individuals haven't got the willpower to avoid such temptation – surely it must be our problem?

If you are one of the millions trying to lose or even just keep a check on your weight and try to fight your willpower each time you see tempting food, you will almost certainly fail. The plain truth of the matter is that the manipulators are so good at getting us to say 'yes' that we are given an enormous amount of 'help' in our food buying – even though we might prefer not to have it.

So many of us live our lives as slaves to our taste buds, aided and abetted by the food giants: they know that if something is made to taste good we will probably eat it, even though we may possibly feel guilty about doing so later.

David knew what he was up against when he took on Goliath. But in our society we, the small consumers, are effectively fighting a well-equipped army of food manufacturing and retailing Goliaths. They are fiercely competitive amongst each other but we are the ones who get pushed around by them. At least David could see the giant in front of him. We only see their carefully constructed warm and friendly images which disguise razor-sharp business expertise and a devotion to extracting every penny they can from a mainly unsuspecting quarry. Most of us are totally unaware of the extent of this manipulation. Research has proved that we each spend up to 25 per cent more than we need to when we go food shopping. The manufacturers and retailers claim that their profit margins are low but by increasing the amount of money we spend they can dramatically increase their overall profitability.

When you stop to calculate the number of times each of us goes shopping and then consider the sheer numbers of shoppers, you can begin to see how so many of the massive food conglomerates are able to announce such staggering profits each year.

> ## British Food Manufacturing Turnover and Profits[1]
>
> *Unilever*: Total sales: £23,163 million. Pre-tax profits: £1,792 million (NB: Food sales represent 52% of total business)
>
> *Grand Metropolitan*: Total sales: £8,748 million. Pre-tax profits: £963 million
>
> *Associated British Foods*: Total sales: £4,877 million. Pre-tax profits: £4,647 million
>
> *Dalgety*: Total sales: £3,769 million. Pre-tax profits: £1,109 million
>
> *Cadbury Schweppes*: Total sales: £3,232 million. Pre-tax profits: £3,164 million

These profits are the combined result of efficiency, professionalism and precision on a military scale, alleged over-pricing of some products, cut-throat buying from their suppliers and, most importantly, some of the most detailed and accurate research material available on shoppers. The computerized information at their disposal about us is absolutely awesome.

Procter & Gamble is the world's largest purchaser of television advertising, closely followed in the rankings by many of the food giants. All of them feed us continually with images of their products. Irrespective of whether we have ever bought particular items, after such repetition on television many of the foods they manufacture become an integral part of our lives. It is then a small step for us actually to buy them. Food manufacturers think in the long term – they know they are going to be in business for a very long time and recognize that if they hit us over the head for long enough, eventually we will buy from them. Maybe we won't buy all of their products all of the time, but for many reasons we will consistently pick up their brand instead of a competitor's. In order for us to do this they will use every device and technique; they will make us laugh, try to blind us with science or appeal to our deepest insecurities and anxieties all in a concerted effort to attract our attention, persuade us to pick up their product, make a positive judgement on it, put it into our shopping trolley and pay for it.

Retailers sell everything which can satisfy our nutritional needs – fresh, high quality produce. But food retailers cannot help selling just about *any* food which they feel enough people would be prepared to buy. They are *not* in the business of taking responsibility for our nutrition. It is up to us as individuals to ensure that the nutritionally 'empty' foods on display do not account for too high a proportion of our diet.

Because we are creatures of habit, millions of people buy food without thinking too much about what they are doing. Manufacturers and retailers know this, too. We wander along the aisles of supermarkets in a trance-like state, jarred back to reality only when we see the final bill at the checkout.

Taste

We are invariably sold on the 'taste' qualities of food. This is the most widely used and easiest technique to provoke us into buying a particular food. Each time we see something described as *tasty, delicious, scrumptious, full of flavour, mouthwatering, appetizing* or *savoury* our saliva glands have become conditioned to get to work immediately, while those tiny taste-buds of ours start sending frantic requests to the brain saying things like, 'Yeah – let's go for *that!*'

Appetizing photographs complete the effect; the food shown is not necessarily the actual food inside the package – it is aimed to look the way we would like it to be. The photographers who take these shots tend to specialize in photographing food – they are highly skilled at making food look as delicious as possible. Look in any glossy consumer magazine. It is no accident that the food photos are so sharp and in focus – you can almost pick them up off the page and put them straight in your mouth.

Manufacturers look continually for new ways to prompt us into 'a buying action'. Notice how many exotic (and more expensive) types of food have been introduced in recent years. Our multi-cultural society has seen an explosion of ethnic foods being made available. These new and stronger taste sensations offer yet more profit potential. Our seemingly insatiable desire for food with more and more flavour is being taken further and further – but where will it all end?

Hundreds of millions of packets of potato crisps are sold each year. We buy them when we are feeling a bit hungry – as something to 'fill the gap' before a more substantial meal. However, these savoury snacks are incapable of doing this because their actual bulk is so insignificant. These products are designed to pack as much flavour on to the surface area of the crisp as possible. The flavours are deliberately strong to titillate your taste buds, yet they do little to satisfy hunger. Once you have finished a bag you are invariably still hungry. The results:

> Food Content: 1, Taste: 5
> Nutrition: 0, Profit: 7

No discussion of the palatability of food as a sales technique would be complete without a brief look at how we are encouraged to stuff our faces with chocolate at every opportunity.

From an early age we are taught that if we are 'good' we will be rewarded with chocolate or sweets. By the time we have reached adulthood we are fully conditioned into associating a bar of chocolate with 'spoiling' ourselves. It becomes a conditioned reflex; feeding brings comfort. The confectionery industry knows this and plays on it every chance they get. They also invest in making sure that today's children have learned to want chocolate. Unwittingly we as parents give the chocolate-makers a lot of help by perpetuating what we were brought up on: 'If you are good, you'll be rewarded with some chocolate!'

Marketers in the confectionery business have developed all sorts of ways to overcome any reluctance we might have in indulging ourselves with their products. A box of chocolates, for example, has been designed to allow you to take just one or two pieces before putting the box away for another time. The trouble is, from their research they know we don't do that – the majority of us open the box and scoff the lot! Chocolate is sold as delicious and energy-providing rather than as a 'food' with little nutritional value that gives us spots, rots our teeth, makes us feel guilty about eating it in the first place and, in time, contributes to obesity and its accompanying health risks such as heart disease. It is a mark of how successful the persuaders are that they manipulate and encourage us successfully to eat tens of millions of bars every year.

This is partially achieved by manufacturers and retailers ensuring that they provide the maximum number of opportunities and outlets to buy their products. Chocolate is now so widely distributed that the precise moment we feel 'peckish' we are usually within a very short distance from a retailer or vending machine to satisfy that impulse. And by keeping the price relatively low we can spoil ourselves easily, cheaply and regularly.

You will have noticed that chocolates are often displayed at supermarket checkouts. The impulse to buy is very strong, especially if you (and your children) are standing in the queue waiting to pay for the rest of your shopping. Retailers know that a significant proportion of customers will give in to temptation. Even if you can control the urge to spoil yourself, your children – trainee consumers – will pester you for long enough so you give in to them 'just for a quiet life'. If this happens those retailers have beaten you again!

Even though children are not responsible for buying the foods they eat, they play a significant role in what their parents buy for them. Food manufacturers use all sorts of techniques to help children 'direct' their parents towards certain products.

TV commercials featuring cartoon characters and catchy music jingles are often aimed specifically at children. Packs of breakfast cereal containing cards or small toys promote brand loyalty to make sure Mum and Dad don't switch brands. Food manufacturers often pay large sums for the rights to adorn their packages with popular children's cartoon heroes. They have to pay more to process the food into the shapes of these characters, but if it makes the food more 'fun' to eat, they will happily pay it.

The food industry has become so powerful they can lobby governments and dictate terms to the media. It has been known for them to withdraw or threaten to withdraw their advertising if they dislike or disapprove of editorial content. This happens quite a lot in the US; it is highly likely it will happen more and more in Britain, too. The industry moguls know that food already represents a third of all retail sales and a fifth of all consumer spending.

I may be accused of being too harsh a judge of their methods and behaviour; after all, they would argue, they have dramatically improved the quality, variety and availability of food. However, these 'plus' points do not detract from the fact that they are responsible for the widespread manipulation of a population that has been fooled into believing it makes its own choices.

Scientific food research is constantly progressing as it combines and re-combines natural flavours, colours, smells and textures as well as developing new and synthetic flavours. The best of these new chemicals will be incorporated into our future foods. They have now reached such sophistication that in tests consumers will even prefer the chemical flavours to the originals they have set out to duplicate. We end up with bland tasting food.

Retailers can get very 'jumpy' with journalists if they feel a report will reveal too much about how they operate. Only recently I was filming an item on location about 'shopping trends'. There was nothing controversial about the report and the director wanted me to deliver my script in front of a supermarket – it didn't matter which one. We found a suitable location nearby, but the moment we set up our camera outside this well-known supermarket chain store we were confronted by a manager, who asked us firmly to leave. Apparently it was head office's policy to prohibit all 'unauthorized' filming. She also confided that they had been subject to a number of embarrassing reports in the past.

Are You a Reconstituted Hamburger?

We rarely take time to realize that if we eat junk, we become junk. Eating is seen as such an obvious and basic human function that we often let it 'take care of itself'. In reality, this means accepting blindly whatever we are manipulated into eating. If we are persuaded to eat food that is not good for us, it is easy to see that eventually we will become overweight, unfit and unhealthy.

If you are going to be in control of your life, being in charge of your body and what you eat is absolutely essential. To do this we need to go back to some basic issues.

What you eat, how much you eat and how often you eat is your responsibility – no one else's.

If you allow such an important responsibility to be handed over to a third party, you have to accept the consequences. I hope that what you have read so far in this chapter will make it easier for you to see how you can regain control of what you eat in the future. In Chapter 1 I made the analogy that life is a bit like driving an automobile. Your body can be thought of in a similar way. You can either go through life lovingly looking after it, or you can hammer the hell out of it, mistreating it, never cleaning or polishing it or caring whether it's up to the job of carrying you through to old age.

No one with any sense would even consider filling a car with contaminated or poorly manufactured fuel. If this was done just once the engine would certainly run badly, fuel lines would get blocked and the car's performance would deteriorate. Depending on how contaminated the fuel was, the engine might be destroyed or require extensive repair work.

Our bodies are far more complicated than the most advanced high-performance engines. Yet every day for our entire lives millions of us think nothing of feeding ourselves with whatever fuel is available, regardless of its quality. Small wonder that so many of us suffer from digestive problems.

Junk food, as its name implies, contains few, if any valuable nutrients and is designed specifically to deliver the maximum taste sensation – notice how most burgers, for example, are a clever combination of soft, doughy bread (easy to bite into), often with seeds, tasty relishes and mayonnaise (to make you lick your lips or fingers), highly flavoured cheeses, crisp lettuce (providing a psychological 'freshness') and pickles for an additional tangy taste. Each ingredient is chosen carefully to make the most of a 'constructed' taste and texture for the 'food'.

Every aspect of the junk food business is geared towards increasing sales and profitability: nothing escapes scrutiny. Even the seating in fast food restaurants is researched; it is deliberately designed to be uncomfortable so the customer is less likely to want to stay for too long. This way they increase their turnover of customers – without ever asking anyone to leave!

Have you ever noticed that soon after you have eaten a large fast-food meal you feel just as hungry as you did before? Maybe your brain is telling you that it wants some 'real' food – not the rubbish you have just filled your stomach with? Invariably we will reach for more junk food to satisfy the hunger. Shortly afterwards we feel hungry again – for the same reason. It becomes a vicious circle. Our poor bodies are trying hard to extract as much goodness from whatever we feed them with.

In contrast, if you make a habit of eating fresh, wholesome food you break out of the eating cycle I have just described. It is so easy to forget that everything we eat and drink has to be processed by our bodies. The more we burden our digestive system with foods that have little or no nutritional value, the more energy we waste. We desperately need this energy if we are to lead effective and productive lives.

This might start to sound as if you should never do anything unless it is sensible and 'controlled' – not at all. There are occasions when you should lose a bit of control, be spontaneous and enjoy yourself – if it means eating and drinking more than you might normally, so be it. It's your life, live it the way you think best. What I am trying to explain is how we fall into self-destructive patterns as a result of outside pressures and persuasion from those who want us to eat particular foods – for their benefit, not ours. By understanding the basics of how the food you eat affects your body you can learn to control an area of your life that is the source of so much unhappiness for millions of people throughout the world.

Think of the times when you have overeaten and drunk too much in the past – possibly at Christmas or Thanksgiving. It is highly likely that soon afterwards you felt tired and lethargic. This is because your body needs to go into overdrive trying to break all that food down. It has a massive and highly complex 'sorting out' job to do – taking out all the 'good' bits to use as fuel and casting aside the waste. No wonder you feel exhausted the morning after a large night-time meal! Your body has been working all night trying to digest it all. And you thought you were resting. The simple answer is to stop eating large meals late at night, or better still, stop eating large meals entirely! It has been reported that because of the quantity and the wide variety of food types consumed at such a meal, digestion of Christmas lunch can still be going on by New Year's Day. For all that time the food is lying inside you at body temperature, starting to decompose. This explains why you might feel somewhat 'delicate' for a while after such meals.

Simply by controlling the way you eat it is possible to improve radically the quality of your life. If you are seriously interested in changing the way you eat I cannot recommend highly enough a best-selling book called *Fit for Life* by Harvey and Marilyn Diamond. When I read it some years ago it improved my life instantly by totally changing my approach to food. It will be of interest to everyone, even those who do not want or need to lose weight. I lost 1½ stone simply by changing *what* I ate and *how* and *when* I ate it. Much of my thinking about food is based on what I learned from this book and from the Hay diet (on which the book is based).

By following this style of eating I broke away from many of today's conventions relating to food. I no longer felt deprived of any of the foods I had previously regarded as favourites.

Believe me, walking past a cake shop or a kiosk selling chocolate used to be a problem for me – but not any more. Nowadays I simply tell myself that the chocolate-laden gateaux temptingly displayed in the window are specifically designed to look as appealing as possible to make me want to buy them. I refuse to allow the retailer to persuade me. This in turn has the effect of making me feel empowered and leads to a sense of 'knowing' that I am in control of my own body. After a while you too will learn to realize that just because something is so available – you don't have to say 'yes', nor do you need to feel as though you are 'going without' when you say 'no'.

If it helps, each time you buy any food, or next time you are on the verge of buying a tasty snack, ask yourself who will derive the most benefit from your purchase: you or the manufacturer? This will often stop you buying an unnecessary snack. Also, never go food shopping when you are hungry!

Try the following experiment when you next go food shopping: work out for yourself how many of the foods on display are sold purely on 'taste'. Then look closely at some of the labels of these foods to see how many contain added flavourings and added sugar. The population has acquired a sweet tooth because of the sheer volume of sugar added to many of our most common processed foods. Even a tin of baked beans has added sugar.

Losing Weight

A recent young woman's lifestyle magazine survey concluded that 6 out of 10 of its readers thought of themselves as overweight. Its findings also showed that 7 out of 10 were currently on a diet. It is highly likely that the majority of these women are not overweight in the clinical sense.

That same magazine was probably partly responsible for their feelings of dissatisfaction with their bodies in the first place. We have been brainwashed into believing that we have to be slim to look our best. I am not suggesting that we should not try to look after ourselves, but it is important to understand why so many feel the need to lose weight.

On the one hand we are encouraged to *eat, eat, eat*. Then, when we have done so, we are told by society that we are overweight, fat slobs. Overeating is encouraged by the food industry. Portion sizes are carefully researched. They want us to feel 'full' because if a portion is too small, consumers may not buy again. Our parents are also guilty of teaching us at an early age to eat more than we may need. We must not waste food. I'm sure everyone is familiar with 'Eat everything on your plate, or you won't get any pudding and you won't grow up to be big and strong like daddy.' We are constantly offered opportunities to over-indulge. For example, at salad bars we have become so adept at piling our plates so high with food they become a feat of engineering and balance. It could be turned into an Olympic sport.

We allow ourselves to be sold foods that destroy our figures, give us spots, bulges and depression, only to be persuaded to accept commercially motivated 'help' to shed this excess poundage. It is also paradoxical that in the past 30 years or so, as food has become more widely distributed there is now more widespread obesity than ever before. It seems to be more of a problem in one of the world's most affluent countries, the US. As a direct result of this obesity the US is the birthplace of countless fad diets.

Because of the nature of our 'now' society, we are fed the message that everything is instantly available. Don't be fooled by anyone who tries to sell you on the idea of immediate weight loss. Such an approach is a proven *business* technique to persuade you to say 'yes' to their proposition. They know that if they can persuade someone who is overweight to believe that they are far closer to looking at their best, that person will be more likely to commit to their lucrative diet.

Those who get sucked into believing such nonsense invariably pay their money, fail and feel worse about what they see as *their* inability to become more attractive, which then leads to more feelings of low self-worth. The majority of customers of the 'instant' merchants will fall by the wayside, or if they do lose the weight promised they invariably put it back on – with interest.

The ultimate aim for anyone who is serious about reducing his or her weight is 1) to lose it, 2) to keep it off and 3) to be able to eat well in the future. So, think about this: if it took two years to put on excess weight, at least two years should be set aside to lose it. By changing fundamentally your approach to losing weight it becomes so much easier. As someone who has lost a substantial amount of weight by this method I can verify that it works. Once I learned to recognize the many different ways the food manufacturers and retailers were trying to persuade me to eat their products, I found it easier to say 'no'. By deliberately slowing down the time it takes to lose weight, the unrealistic pressure to gain an immediate result fades away. If losing weight is not worth all this effort – do yourself a favour – stop wasting your time getting upset about it, decide to forget about going on a diet and get on with your life.

If enjoying short-term food and alcohol 'binges' or 'highs' is more important to you than long-term good health, that is your decision. Although more often than not, overindulgence or overconsumption is never planned – it is simply the result of repeatedly accepting and then consuming what we are offered. Could it be that obese people are simply more susceptible to the efforts of the persuaders?

Many people who try to lose weight do so because they feel they should. They are under pressure from their family and friends. Dieting for the benefit of others won't work either. Don't bother trying to lose any weight unless *you* want to. Ask yourself why you *really* want to lose it. Are you bowing to pressure from the image merchants or do you have clear reasons for doing something about it? If you see that being less overweight will have worthwhile and noticeable advantages to you professionally, socially and personally – do it. When you know the answer to these questions, losing weight will be easier. Notice I didn't say 'easy' – it's never easy.

We are what we eat. Whatever goes into our mouths affects our appearance, attitudes, feelings and health. Our food-buying and eating habits have become automatic. By regaining control over these fundamental parts of our lives we can make a considerable improvement to our future happiness and well-being.

[1] Institute of Grocery Distribution, 1991

5

Television and the Media

Are you one of the hundred of millions who, on a daily basis, switch off as you switch on? Television (or the 'one-eyed monster' as it is sometimes called) has become the centre-point of so many people's lives. Not even John Logie Baird could have predicted how his invention would change the lives of so many so fundamentally.

I would like to ask you to look upon your television set in a different way.

Average television viewing in Britain is approximately 3½ hours per person per day. In the US this figure is higher. The British figures multiply thus: 24½ hours per week, 98 hours per month, 1,277 hours per year. By the time a teenager reaches the age of 18 he or she will have watched an average of 19,162 hours of television. This figure is based on 15 years' viewing to ensure it is low as possible. As children tend to watch more TV than the population as a whole, this rough calculation is deliberately rather conservative. And 19,162 hours viewing is equivalent to 798 days or *two years!* By the time these same individuals reach the age of 80, they will have spent the equivalent of about 10 solid years watching television.

Television will literally steal your life if you allow it to. Often, the television set is the first electrical device young children learn to switch on for themselves. It becomes their constant 'electronic babysitter' during the early part of their lives. When they are old enough to look after themselves, many still just sit there, passively watching a conveyor-belt full of televisual images.

It has been estimated that the average 18-year-old has seen over 500,000 TV commercials. Further estimations indicate they will also see up to 15,000 fake deaths and mutilations plus a wide array of sexually-based violence, countless 'exciting' scenes of violence to property, car-chase wrecks, buildings being blown up, etc. All this stimulation is absorbed by passive, uninvolved viewers of all ages.

We are deliberately misled by the TV companies into believing that television is an inexpensive, value-for-money entertainment and information service. They tell us about how they provide such a wide variety of news, drama, sport, comedy and game shows, music and educational documentaries – but their glowing descriptions of their own work hides the truth.

The reality is that television is the most powerful *sales* medium ever developed. Everything you see on commercial television is broadcast to persuade you to sit in front of it for as long and as often as possible so that you watch the maximum number of advertisements.

It is easy to describe the television programmes we have grown to love as merely something the TV companies choose to give away!

British television boasts the highest quality programming in the world, constantly reminding us of the numerous awards the TV industry confers on itself. There seems to be a category for every type of programme, performer, technician, commercial, programme trailer, graphics sequence, sound effects, editing, etc. The list goes on. But it is also true that television is switched on by many just for subdued room lighting!

All TV companies want our time and attention and will do whatever they can to persuade us to give in to their requests. Many programmes are made using a strict 'format' or formula – quiz and games shows, situation comedies, populist drama and soap operas are produced in this tried and tested way. Programme trailers are similarly designed and scheduled to excite, intrigue and amuse you into staying in front of that TV. They also share another function – to fill airtime. Television companies are always juggling with the constant need to fill their airtime as cheaply as possible while ensuring they do not force viewers to switch off, or worse than that, switch over to another channel.

In the US especially, the end-credits of each programme are scrolled across the screen at lightning speed. Many advertisers want to dispense with them entirely because they have found that large numbers of viewers switch channels before the commercials come on. Partially to counteract this 'disgraceful' behaviour by viewers, voiceovers are used to promote the next programme while the credits are still rolling – in an attempt to keep viewers glued to the screen.

During four years as a BBC continuity announcer, my job involved writing scripts to persuade the highest number of people to watch the BBC's programmes. My colleagues (and counterparts on competing stations) assembled the most eye-catching promotional trailers to make the upcoming programmes appear as enticing as possible. There are countless stories of colleagues choosing specific snippets of, for example, situation comedies, only to be told off by the producers for showing 'the only funny part of the entire show'!

Study the trailers yourself when you next watch television. Ask yourself: who benefits most if you decide to watch those programmes? The TV companies will never tell you openly that they need you to watch, but if they are to make money they certainly do.

BBC television (and public broadcasting stations, or PBS in the US) are somewhat different to more commercial stations in that they have to persuade large numbers of people to watch their programmes or risk extinction. In recent years the BBC has changed fundamentally what used to be their rather elitist approach to broadcasting, now developing and producing programmes aimed at the largest audience.

Commercial television has a constant battle on its hands to maintain and (wherever possible) increase their viewing figures. Independent research organizations such as Nielson or BARB monitor our viewing using a variety of methods. The figures they publish have far-reaching implications, resulting in instant death for some programmes that show a consistent drop in their audience figures. In the US it has been known for highly popular shows to be cancelled immediately because they lost a point or two in the ratings. To hell with the fact that a lot of people like the programmes – if the TV company is failing to make enough money – it could get cut from the network.

Audience figures are *so* important because they are used as the basis for selling commercial airtime to advertising agencies. Not all advertisers want to reach the highest audiences – as discussed in Chapter 4, they target their adverts to particular groups. Whatever programmes interest you, there will be advertisers willing to pay vast sums to reach you and others like you. Their detailed research tells them which programmes you are most likely to watch.

The major television networks and their advertisers would be thrilled if you sat watching TV for the majority of your time. Thankfully for them, millions already do. The television set is switched on first thing in the morning and is watched constantly throughout the day and late into the evening. This happens every day in a significant number of households.

Programmes

Television companies are keen to ensure that such viewing habits continue. They achieve this by making watching as easy as possible. They will quite obligingly supply a constant stream of programmes that don't require much mental effort. Game shows, soap operas, situation comedies, even news programmes are presented in an easy-to-digest form so that collapsing in front of the TV is a pleasant and convenient way to spend a few hours 'relaxing'. They fill the day with programmes to keep you company and stay watching. Research has shown that some people feel guilty watching TV during the day. To overcome this, daytime programmes are filled with items about cookery, improving your lifestyle and personal fitness – anything that makes it easier for you to justify watching.

Movie subscription channels generate a significant proportion of revenue for satellite operators, while 'terrestrial' TV operators have known for a long time that they can pull in large numbers of viewers for blockbuster movies. Showing movies not only costs less but is an assured way of attracting high audiences. Most importantly, movies guarantee an audience for up to two hours or more, ensuring the audience sees a large number of commercials. Movies are routinely edited (or these days shortened electronically) so as to allow TV companies to insert more advertisements.

Many movies are put on TV at about 10.30 p.m. The schedulers have discovered that if they can persuade us to start watching a movie we are likely to stay with it, even past midnight. Once again they will have succeeded in manipulating us into seeing more commercials. They know that if they scheduled shorter programmes at this late hour the end of each programme would provide too many people with the opportunity to switch off and go to bed. That would never do! So what if you feel exhausted in the morning?

New programmes are manufactured to fit pre-set durations. In the US, new shows undergo extensive pre-testing to ensure they appeal to the widest possible audience. Many years ago while on a visit to New York City, I attended such a test session. The entire audience sat in specially designed seats, each equipped with a number of buttons. We were asked to press a green button each time we saw something we liked and a red button when we saw something we did not like. After the screening we were asked to fill in a ten-page questionnaire about our TV viewing habits. We were then interviewed about the programme we had just seen. A by-product of all this audience research is bland, diluted programming that nevertheless delivers consistently high audiences and therefore higher advertising revenues.

Many television programme makers produce material in deliberately short 'packages' – taking into consideration what they perceive to be our inability to concentrate for more than three or four minutes. We have been taught to have 'butterfly minds', to flit from one activity to another without staying long enough to get too involved.

Television must be at least partially responsible for the widespread apathy, docility and boredom in our society. Programmes for teenagers and other young people in particular tend to concentrate on fast action, quick-fire editing and visual effects – cramming as much stimulation as possible into the shortest amount of time. If a programme is too slow, the viewer is likely to reach for the remote channel changer or the fast forward control. Our stimulation must be instant, just like our coffee. No wonder reality seems so slow, and dull, by comparison.

Most people fail to understand exactly how they are manipulated into spending their lives in front of the screen. Much of my time is spent among people whose lives are devoted to television. If they are not working on a programme they are watching everybody else's, purely to keep up to date with what is going on in the industry. Few television people accept that there is anything more important in life. But I will always remember one time when I was filming on location. Chatting casually to the guy in charge of rigging the lights, I asked him whether he had seen a particular documentary the previous night. He said he didn't own a television set. I could not believe that someone who earned his living from television did not own a TV set. He went on to say 'I am so busy living my own life that I have chosen not to spend it watching others living theirs!'

To be one of life's players requires effort, but as watching TV is carefully engineered to require so little, it is the easy option. It's no wonder TV has become such a widespread, daily, international habit.

News

We are led to believe that knowing what is going on in the world is important. But is it so important that we listen or watch the news at breakfast, read a morning paper on the train going to work, watch the news at lunchtime, read an evening paper on the way home, then tune into the TV news before we go to bed? And on Sundays we wade through mountains of newsprint. We have become news junkies, rarely missing opportunities to watch, listen to or read about what is happening at home and in other people's lives throughout the world.

Surely, such mass consumption of news is taking 'watching others living their lives' to extremes? Countless men and women spend at least an hour and a half every day being told what others are doing. Wouldn't it be a bit more interesting if they spent at least some of that time dedicated to doing something with their own lives? Make a decision about how important the news is for you; deliberately ration your 'intake' if necessary.

News is often obsessed with murder, terrorism, rape, war, famine, scandal, political corruption, disease and poverty. We have been conditioned in this 'fast forward' society of ours to expect pace and excitement in everything seen on TV, including the news. The news must be punchy. It often conveys forced urgency. Many of the subjects treated to a 'hard' news approach are often, on closer inspection, far more mundane than we are led to believe.

There is no room in the tabloid press for the understated. Shock tactics sell papers. We are swept along in a tide of 'created' and stage-managed stimulation and titillation. Rupert

Murdoch's *Sun* newspaper takes this titillation into soft-porn territory with the daily 'tit and bum' photo on page three.

This reminds me of a story involving some American TV reporters and their first encounter with this type of tabloid newspaper. When I was reading the news for BBC Breakfast television in London we were visited by the Governor of Colorado on a tour promoting the tourist attractions of his state. He was accompanied by two reporters from competing TV stations in Denver. When I showed them a copy of the *Sun*'s page 3, they practically fell off their seats. They found it difficult to accept that British authorities would allow photos of a topless 'glamour girl' to be published every day in something purporting to be a newspaper. I cannot imagine what they would have said about *The Daily Sport*.

The truth is that such news 'comics' achieve massive sales. It would not be commercially appropriate or viable for Murdoch to publish the same format in the US where instead of making hefty profits he would be hit hard by the large advertisers, who would immediately exert their clout by withdrawing their ads. 'Morality' groups might even boycott his other media interests.

This merely serves to illustrate precisely how commercial motives govern the media. Nor is it fair to pick out Murdoch in particular: every media mogul and advertiser will do whatever he or she can to generate profit.

It is worth taking a closer look at how a typical tabloid newspaper is compiled. Large headlines and full-page photographs cost relatively little to produce. Easy-to-digest news stories are featured alongside a high proportion of media-related stories: television programme listings, previews, reviews, celebrity photos and public relations 'puffery'. Much of this material is readily supplied to the newspapers, often free of charge, by PR departments from TV and film production companies. Every day, they fill page after page and serve as a constant reminder to their readers to watch television.

Newspapers and television have created an image of mutual disdain, but in reality they have a parasitic relationship. Television helps to fill countless newspaper pages, while newspaper reports are invariably used as source material for numerous TV news and current affairs programmes. The combined effect is one of keeping our attention.

As for other material included in the news, we are led to believe that it is always both impartial and accurate. Anyone you meet who has first-hand knowledge of any news story will tell you that, regardless of whether the story was featured in 'quality' or tabloid papers, on radio or television, invariably there are glaring inaccuracies. Some cannot be helped but others are deliberate attempts to 'spice' up a story that might otherwise appear too mundane. More accurately put, it has to be tampered with (but only slightly!) to give it an appropriate 'angle'. In the case of individual stories this tampering is so slight as to be almost insignificant – but when it happens again and again throughout all areas of the news, we are left with a much-distorted image of real life.

It is widely known within the TV industry that one particular news cameraman who covers wars all over the world has, as part of his camera 'kit', a small child's doll. It has been known for this cameraman to position the doll carefully in the foreground of a scene showing the remains of a recent urban battle. That doll has been seen at more wars than Bob Hope!

On a serious note, such behaviour is grossly manipulative. It is designed to evoke particular feelings in us. It is only fair to say that this behaviour is rare and not representative of most news organizations.

Television packs as many 'jolts per minute' into its output – to the point where it numbs our sensitivities. News coverage of terrorist attacks and murders are commonplace – we see the carnage of war and the suffering faces of those living with drought, famine and dire poverty. We become accustomed and hardened to it. 'Good' news loses audiences and makes newspaper circulations plummet. Only by rationing your intake of news can you cut down on the number of depressing images you have to process – images that can seriously affect the way you feel about yourself.

The argument that 'It happens, so we should know about it' is a weak one. Just because it is technically possible to get close-ups of atrocities and to use satellites to beam the pictures back to the news studio from remote parts of the world, to be shown 'live', does not mean that it *must* be done. But if a TV company has paid large sums for such state-of-the art technical facilities, it is more inclined to make maximum use of such material. This is in part why we are given exhaustive coverage of 'major' news stories such as wars, elections and national disasters. Blanket coverage is more cost-effective for the news supplier. Populist journalism is not interested in 'making a difference': it concentrates on filling airtime in the most 'entertaining' way.

Manipulation in the news is far more widespread than most people realize, although I will state that after nearly 10 years working in radio and television I have *never* encountered a journalist who angles the news to suit his or her own political views. Yet journalists are having to resort more and more to using outside sources such as public relations consultancies. These well-resourced teams of highly skilled professionals supply the media with all types of stories, interviewees, statistics and photo opportunities. Journalists *try* to eliminate those stories that are blatant attempts at promoting a politically or commercially motivated view, but they are often working under such pressure that it is difficult for them to keep an overview of the larger picture.

The volume and quality of media exposure is monitored constantly by every political party, each one poised to shout 'foul' if it feels it is not being given equal coverage. The next time you see a politician on television you can be assured he or she is there as part of a carefully organized campaign aimed solely at swaying public opinion towards his or her political party, or alternatively to 'rubbish' the efforts of the opposition. And politicians are often used as guests in documentaries and studio discussion programmes purely because they will usually participate for free – for the publicity and exposure.

Politicians are coached extensively on how to conduct themselves in all areas of the media. Much of this media manipulation has been learned and adapted from the US, where political stage-management has approached art-form status for decades. Political advisers have known for a long time that a candidate's appearance and performance plays a bigger part in getting him or her elected to power than any actual capacity for the job. We, the public, are sucked in by appearances all the time.

Few achieve such proficiency as former British Prime Minister Margaret Thatcher. Early photographs show crooked teeth, a lacklustre hairstyle and uninteresting clothes. Her total 'make over' included voice training which lowered the tone of her voice to strengthen her specially created media image even further.

Study for yourself how TV debates are staged. Speakers are chosen carefully for their 'stand' on the issue under discussion. For a debate comprising three guests and one interviewer (known within TV as a 'three-plus-one') notice how the participants are configured in the studio: two guests on, say, the left side of the interviewer, the third immediately on the interviewer's right. The producer hopes that the individual he or she has positioned furthest away will have the strongest, most aggressive views. The person in the middle is there to mediate, while the third person will often be the 'defender' of the issue. Such attention to detail is part of the 'formula' or 'conveyor-belt' nature of television. It ensures a relatively controlled production but it also means rather bland television. All programmes are also timed precisely, so it is highly likely that each viewpoint will be 'produced by stopwatch'; hardly the best environment to make any real headway on an issue.

As for every other programme on television, all have been developed to persuade us to sit there, in a passive and relaxed state (when our defences are down) soaking up the messages in the ad. breaks.

Take soap operas as an example – the cliff-hanger at the end of each episode safely guarantees a substantial and addicted audience for the next time. The more we watch, the more our lives are controlled by it. The weekly television ratings published in the broadcast trade press consistently show that the entire top ten programmes are soap operas. In Britain, up to 15 million viewers will tune in for each and every episode of their favourite soaps. They are all carefully engineered to appeal to the widest cross-section of the public.

TV chat shows are similarly created to appeal to a wide audience. Many of the guests featured on these shows are promoting their latest book, TV show or movie. They will receive a minimal fee to cover basic expenses because such mass exposure is worth a fortune to those who produce their products. For example, movie stars are often required, as part of their contract for a movie they have made, to be available for TV, radio and press interviews – so they get paid by the film company. This offers a good deal to the TV companies; relatively low cost programming which consistently delivers a high audience for advertisers. The guests benefit from prime time exposure, the possibility of higher box office sales, which in turn increases the likelihood of future work for them. Once again – we pay for it all.

Audience figures confirm that millions of people watch TV even when they are not particularly interested in what they are viewing. This was proved by an interesting experiment conducted in Britain. Immediately after the national weather forecast a large number of people were telephoned at random. Those who had just seen the forecast were asked to tell the researcher what it had said. Seventy per cent weren't even close.

What to Do

I am not trying to suggest that you should stop watching television altogether. But if you are serious about wanting to be in control of your life, it is in your best interests to consider carefully the effect television has on you and your family. We have come to believe that if we are offered something then by definition it must be worth having. We accept without taking a moment to question its value and relevance to our lives.

If you decide to cut down on your TV watching, this suggestion might prove helpful: plan your viewing thoroughly in advance. Go through the television listings circling the programmes you think you would like to watch. Then, if you have a video recorder, instead of watching programmes when they are actually on, make a point of recording them to watch later. You will probably find that you won't bother watching a large proportion of what you have recorded. You will only watch the most interesting material – saving you time to devote to other, more fulfilling pursuits.

We know that conversation stops among families all over the world when the television is on. We no longer have the time to get to know those we live with. If we are not watching TV we are talking about it. Television is the single most popular topic of conversation between family and friends – 45 per cent – the second-most popular subject being the cost of living at 41 per cent.[1] Few people realize that both subjects are inextricably linked – as TV advertising is largely responsible for the inflated prices we are charged for the products we buy. I have spent over ten years working in television, often on a daily basis and I have now come to realize that television steals the lives of millions, creating many unattainable 'wants' and 'desires' that viewers would remain immune to if they did not watch so much.

Obviously, not all television is a waste of time: there are many top-quality programmes and there is nothing wrong with wanting to spend the occasional few hours relaxing in front of the TV. The biggest problem is when watching becomes a substitute for living. Anyone who wants control in his or her life must ensure that life doesn't 'just happen'. Taking time to think is the next stage, and the subject of the next chapter.

[1] TOM Attitudes to Advertising Survey

2

Regaining Control

6

No Time to Think?

In previous chapters you have seen the many and varied ways people are manipulated and controlled by others. This basic understanding should enable you to look at your life in a totally new and different way. Immediate benefits should include being able to save money on your shopping bills. You ought now to be able to start identifying the techniques used to persuade you to do things you would not otherwise consider doing. Despite the concerted efforts being made to thwart your attempts, you should be able to achieve a degree of mastery over your impulsiveness. And finally, you can now derive a delicious sense of self-satisfaction in the knowledge that you, unlike many millions of others, *know* what you are being subjected to and are making a conscious decision to stop this domination of your life.

This chapter will take you one step closer towards a happier and more successful future. To achieve maximum control in your life you *must* control your own thinking. However, as you will have seen from previous chapters, your thinking is constantly influenced and in some cases even governed by a variety of outside forces. It is a fact of life that if we are too busy, we stop thinking. Consequently, thinking is often shunted to one side because of what we see as a lack of time to devote to it.

In the commercial world, every effort is made to speed up the selling process by making it easy for us to say 'yes' to products and services. The reason is simple: professional salespeople know that the less time an individual spends thinking about a proposition, the more likely he or she is to say 'yes'. It is therefore in the interests of business to operate in a society that moves at a frenetic pace. The faster the pace, the less time we as individuals will spend thinking about what is in our best long-term interests. Life has become so demanding of our time and attention that we tend to allow others to do some of our thinking for us. The less we think for ourselves, the more likely we are to accept blindly the thoughts of others.

We take more and more of our lives for granted, believing this to be the only way to cope with the many pressures and commitments which take over our time. Research has shown that a significant number of people who change jobs and careers have done so shortly after taking a holiday. It is only while on holiday, away from everyday pressures, that they have time to take stock of their careers and any shortcomings in their lives.

Another reason for the widespread lack of independent thought is the fact that effective thinking can be so damn hard! It takes effort and most of us prefer the easy option. To many, thinking deeply and carefully about something is only ever done when there is no other alternative – for example, when a problem needs solving urgently. Thinking becomes the last resort rather than the first. But without thought, there is no achievement; without achievement there can be little success. Everyone wants the secrets of success: the short-cuts, the quick result. Few are prepared to overcome the problems, pain and headaches involved in trying to think deeply about what they really want in life and how they can achieve it. *The surest way to improve your chances of future success is to increase the amount of time you spend thinking.*

The aim should be to increase the effectiveness of your thinking; merely sitting still pondering about your life is unlikely to achieve much. For any thinking to be effective it must be linked to action.

Ideas

Probably the easiest way to achieve enormous success in life is by coming up with a good, workable idea. History is full of individuals who have simply thought of one idea, put it into action and made their fortune. It is not essential to re-invent the wheel or make a brilliant scientific discovery. So many reputations and fortunes have been built on the most ordinary of ideas.

Percy Shaw was driving home late one night from his local pub in the north of England in dense fog. He could hardly see where he was going – but he knew that on one side of the road was a sheer drop down into the valley below. It was then he thought how helpful rows of reflective glass inserted into the middle of the road would be to help motorists to stay on course. After a little trial and error he successfully designed the 'Cat's Eye'. Within a relatively short time he became a multi-millionaire, just from this one idea.

Let's take Ron Hickman as another example. He is the man who designed the Black and Decker Workmate, the adjustable work bench which has helped millions of do-it-yourselfers around the world. That single idea made him a multi-millionaire too. He has since been responsible for a number of other inventions, but none have quite eclipsed the success of his Workmate.

I am sure you would have to agree that there are very few people incapable of dreaming up such simple ideas for themselves. You too could quite easily think of equally good ideas. All you need to add to your idea is the enthusiasm, confidence and commitment to turn it into reality. But here lies the problem – most people dismiss their own ideas by telling themselves 'If it was that good, why hasn't someone else thought of it?' The fact of the matter is that someone else probably has thought of the same idea but, like you, has dismissed it for the same reason. It's quite common to forget about ideas, only to be reminded of them months or even years later when you discover that someone else had 'your' idea, but did something about it and found that it was a great success. The majority of people tend to undervalue their own intelligence and ideas, but are quite prepared to give others full credit for theirs. Brilliant ideas are being thought of every day, in every corner of the world by people just like you and me.

Good, realistic, workable ideas are absolutely everywhere. They are just waiting to be put into action. Look around you – everything you see from the smallest item to the largest; jewellery, furniture, vehicles, buildings – they all started with someone having an idea. They all start with someone saying something like 'What if we . . . ?

It's a sad fact that we are usually taught *what* to think rather than *how* to think. But there is no mystery attached to creative thinking. For anyone who feels incapable of generating good, realistic and workable ideas, here is a crash course in creativity. All individuals possess some specialized knowledge. Use this expertise to come up with a few good ideas. Remember, ideas come to those who ask questions and to those who refuse to accept the *status quo*. By enquiring 'What would happen if..?', many ideas will be generated. Regardless of what job you have, look closely at it and ask yourself the following questions:

- Why is each task (within your job) done the existing way?
- Are there simpler, quicker, cheaper, more effective and interesting alternatives?
- What are the bottlenecks?
- How could you smooth out the problems?
- How does one task compare with others?
- How does a task contrast?
- What would happen if you did tasks at different times or in a different order?
- What if you changed where you performed a given task?
- How would the task be affected if more (or fewer) people were involved?

- If you are involved in manufacturing, ask what would happen if your products were made larger, smaller, from a different material, in a different colour, upside-down, inside-out, back-to-front or in any combination of these alternatives?

Many ideas revolve around satisfying a need. The world is full of problems; if you can find solutions you may have established the basis for personal success in the future. Many new ideas for products are created simply by combining two separate, existing ideas. For example, in simplistic terms, the automobile was invented by combining the wheel with an internal combustion engine.

With a little practice you will easily start to develop more and more ideas. The more ideas you generate the easier it becomes, the more your confidence grows and the more that thinking becomes fun. As your self-assurance grows ask more and more outrageous 'What if . . . ?' questions. Brainstorming sessions can be highly productive. Set a time limit of, say, 10 minutes. Then, with friends or colleagues, encourage a free flow of ideas – criticize nothing. Even the silliest ideas can be highly useful in stimulating more practical solutions to problems.

It is very important that you get into the habit of writing down your ideas in a notebook. If possible keep it next to your bed: it's where most people seem to get their ideas. By writing them down you will ensure that good ideas won't slip away from you. Once you get into the habit of thinking, ideas will just come to you naturally – you won't even have to try. Your mind is like the rest of your body: if you don't exercise it, it gets flabby. If you gain a reputation for being full of good ideas, you can practically write your own meal ticket for life.

The major factor stopping individuals from suggesting new ideas is a fear of being ridiculed or criticized. This applies whether you are designing new products, writing books, painting pictures or even developing scientific experiments.

Anyone who offers their cheek to others knows that it can be kissed, slapped or ignored. Self-confidence ensures that the prospect of criticism does not stop you from supplying ideas to those around you. Suggesting ideas is a bit like being a sportsperson: no one expects you to score a goal with every shot – but the more shots you aim at goal the more likely you are to increase dramatically the number you score. One thing is for sure: anyone who is afraid to take these shots is not going to score at all!

Directive Thinking

Our thinking influences many aspects of our lives. Generating ideas is only one aspect of this. How we think determines our attitudes and the way we behave. In turn, the way we behave often affects what others think about us. How we are perceived can make a difference to the opportunities we are given in our careers and the friendships and romantic relationships we form. These in turn affect the way we feel about ourselves, our happiness, our sense of well-being and security, our stress and energy levels. And all of these affect the way we think. It is an ongoing process.

Everything, therefore, relies on how and what we think. The trouble is that most people become a by-product of their behaviour rather than the reason for it. Look around you when you walk along a busy street and ask yourself whether most of those you see spend very much time thinking about their future. Are they in control of their lives? Do they know where they are going in life? Do they care enough to do something about it? Most don't bother.

Sadly, thinking is under-utilized. Each of us is equipped with a brain which has a massive capability for processing information, evaluating situations and solving problems, but it is widely believed that most of us fail to use more than 5 per cent of its capacity.

Edward de Bono, the famed authority on the subject, calls

thinking 'the ultimate resource'. He is responsible for introducing the term 'lateral thinking', i.e. the ability to think about a situation or problem from a number of different or opposing perspectives. Applying lateral thinking can often result in bizarre yet inspired solutions to all sorts of problems. He describes an effective thinker thus:

> Someone who is in control of his thinking instead of just drifting from idea to idea, emotion to emotion. He is clear about what he is setting out to do: he can define a thinking task and then set about carrying it out. He has both a clear focus and also a broad view of the situation. He favours wisdom rather than cleverness. He enjoys thinking even when it is not particularly successful. He is confident and decisive but also humble . . . He is constructive rather than critical, the purpose of thinking is to reach a better understanding, decision or course of action: not to prove that he is smarter than someone else.
>
> *De Bono's Thinking Course*

Within the world of motivational training there is 'positive' and 'negative' thinking. I have also encountered 'possibility' thinking, 'probability' thinking, 'stinking' thinking and a number of other kinds! The time has come for me to introduce my own offering: *directive thinking*.

While positive thinking has its place, I cannot help believing that 'looking on the bright side' and seeing the glass as 'half-full instead of half-empty' is no longer enough in today's highly complex world. When most of the respected and successful positive-thinking books were written in the 1920s and 30s by the likes of Dr Norman Vincent Peale and Dale Carnegie, life may have been tougher in some ways but it was also far simpler and slower.

Directive thinking takes up where I believe positive thinking leaves off. But be warned: if you are looking for a magic formula – there isn't one! Directive thinking is simply about exerting discipline over the haphazard nature of our thoughts; focusing thought in such a way that it results in action. Those who organize their thinking in this way are far more likely to lead more productive lives. One of the major stumbling blocks experienced by most people is their inability to control their thinking before embarking on – or during – large-scale projects. It is easy to waste an enormous amount of time idly dreaming of what it would be like to complete these projects rather than just getting on with them. Successful people are able to enjoy and concentrate on the *process* of a task rather than its possible future results and benefits.

Directive thinking can be defined as the thought-process needed to turn goals and ambitions into reality: it is a practical way of channelling your thoughts in the pursuit of the goals *you* feel are most important to you.

Whatever you set out to achieve, think through each and every stage needed to complete the task. Then pick out the smallest task you can complete. Then do it. Directive thinking will help you to break each task down into manageable chunks, thus increasing the likelihood of a successful outcome and yet another personal achievement. All too often large tasks never get started because they can appear too daunting. The way you think about any task will determine how you respond to its challenge.

Imagine you have decided to buy a house in need of major renovation work. This is a task that would put off many individuals. By applying directive thinking, you could break the task down into its many different parts. If you did not know how to go about every aspect of the job you could seek advice from the relevant professionals – architects, surveyors, structural engineers, builders, plumbers, electricians, decorators, etc. Each task would be thought through and given its place within the overall framework of the project. Breaking it down in this way will increase dramatically your chances of eventual success. It also teaches you to set realistic goals and minimizes the chances of getting depressed and discouraged by the enormity of your plans.

I am using directive thinking to write this book. I know how much time I have to complete it and how many words I've been contracted to write. By breaking this down into a daily writing schedule of 800 words I can see clearly that this job can be accomplished in the allotted time frame. A specially-designed 'word chart' allows me to see at a glance how I am progressing. I am confident it will be finished on time. The fact that you are now reading this book proves that directive thinking works!

By using directive thinking you start to initiate change. And nothing can be achieved unless a change is brought about. There is a saying that goes 'By the mile it's a trial, by the inch it's a cinch.' Directive thinking shows you how to change the way you look at all tasks, large or small. As a technique for getting things done directive thinking cannot be beaten. Try it.

The directive thinking approach is fundamentally different to the way in which a particular breed of people lead their lives. I have dubbed them PPOs, or 'Project Prevention Officers'. They are invariably self-appointed and pervade all areas of our lives, social as well as professional. They will jam a spanner in the works wherever and whenever they can, finding ways *not* to do things and generally taking the wind out of the sails of anyone who wants to implement new ideas or start new projects. They are related to the 'Jobsworth' dynasty: those who immediately knock down every idea or proposal with the immortal words 'It's more than my job's worth to let you do that!'

Dealing with such individuals involves drastic action: *avoid them whenever you can.* If all fails in your endeavours to bypass these PPOs and their harmful, depressing and frustrating behaviour – use directive thinking to find a new job. PPOs teach what the former British Prime Minister Lloyd George described as 'poverty of ambition'. Your energy and enthusiasm will be welcomed by others; don't allow anyone to sap your strength in this way.

Being a Good Thinker

Not all thinking is productive. Sometimes individuals think so much they are paralysed into inactivity – their thinking becomes an excuse for action rather than an incentive to it. Thinking is an absolute waste of time unless it is linked in some way to specific action. However, as we live in such a fast-paced world, our thinking is often done too quickly. With little time to evaluate a situation properly, we reach decisions without exploring all possible solutions. After jumping to conclusions, many poor thinkers develop the ability to defend their thinking, often with great energy and intransigence. The more 'intelligent' an individual is, the more likely it is that he or she will think too quickly, taking a variety of mental short cuts to arrive at a decision. They will then use their superior intellect and reasoning ability to justify their thoughts, decisions and actions. This can lead to a degree of arrogance in their thinking. The irony is that someone with less intelligence can actually be a better thinker than these arrogant types, because he or she is more inclined to take the time to collate, evaluate and digest all available information before making a decision.

Another source of wasted thinking is getting embroiled in the cut-and-thrust of debate. Gaining a better understanding of issues is obviously a good thing, but when a discussion becomes an opportunity for individuals to apply their skills of rhetoric to a viewpoint they refuse to question, no one wins. Nowhere is there a better example of this kind of wasted thinking than in politics. Politicians all over the world seem to believe that any policy proposed by members of opposing parties must, by definition, be wrong. This is absurd: rarely is any idea or suggestion totally ill-conceived. Rather than conceding what is good about an idea, society tends to endorse the attitude whereby each side will do what it can to destroy whatever has been put forward by any other individual or organization. This is also a serious problem in business. Such behaviour is a criminal waste of everyone's time and effort.

Because criticizing the efforts and ideas of others is so easy it has become an accepted part of our lives – so much so that professional critics can be found everywhere. There is a saying that 'No one ever erected a monument to a critic.' Intellectually it is the easy option to take an opposing viewpoint just for the sake of it. Professional critics serve a number of purposes: to fill airtime and pages of newsprint, to stir up controversy and to provide a kick start for further time-wasting debate, thus filling more airtime and pages!

In the context of 'controlling' your own life, listening to criticism and criticizing others are activities to be avoided at all costs. Refuse to be part of conversations that criticize others – find something more worth while to do with your time.

A good thinker is prepared to listen to those around him or her without feeling the need to interrupt or use the time while others are speaking to formulate the 'clever' things he or she is going to say next. Good thinkers develop the habit of asking meaningful questions designed to increase their knowledge of a subject. Questions should not be used to show off your own knowledge or to put others down.

People who do not think for themselves are prime targets for manipulation. Those who actively and deliberately devote time to thinking about their present and future, consciously linking their ideas with positive action, will gain a significant increase of control and happiness in their lives.

Self-Confidence and Happiness

In my late teens and throughout my twenties I kept a dark secret from my friends. I was troubled by the feeling that there was something terribly wrong with me. I found myself attracted to something I had been led to believe was totally unacceptable for someone with my background. I was afraid of what others might say. These days it is more socially acceptable to admit to it, but at that time it posed serious questions for me – and it's still a brave man who admits it publicly. My problem? I liked country music: I found myself wanting to listen to the likes of Kenny Rogers, Don Williams, Crystal Gayle and Dolly Parton. I just couldn't help it!

It doesn't seem to matter that country music is hugely popular all over the world; it is still thought by many to be music for 'old folks'. This, as anyone who knows anything about it will tell you, is absolute rubbish. But my point is that we live in a society in which it can be difficult to be publicly confident about our personal likes and dislikes.

Even now, in my thirties, if I admit this preference in the 'wrong' quarters I risk ridicule. Indeed, a colleague read an earlier draft of this chapter and scoffed at my 'country confessional', adding, '. . . and I always thought you had better taste!'

This light-hearted example has a deeper significance when applied to personal control. As such it is worth taking a closer look at it. Why is it so widespread and acceptable to mock others for their likes and dislikes? We should be able to enjoy what we like despite what anybody else thinks. We should be free to choose our own preferences in all areas of our lives.

As we get older, of course, we tend to care less about what others think. We learn to accept our own idiosyncrasies, likes and dislikes. But in our early teens few of us are so confident. It is crucially important to 'fit in', to be part of the crowd, even to belong to a gang; all this to gain acceptance and friendship. Throughout our lives we will always seek approval; as teenagers we tend to be more afraid to express our own personal likes and dislikes in case they are found 'unacceptable' by our circle of 'friends'. So, rather than risk being treated as an outcast, many of us as teenagers suppress our own preferences.

Young people are fed so many images and conflicting messages that it is easy for them to become confused and unsure about what they think. They are told constantly what they *should* think and how to behave, and the so-called 'style' rules can change so quickly.

The popular music scene is a perfect example of how marketing experts make the most of teenage insecurities. Young people are provided with a wide choice of carefully moulded singers and bands, each with a particular image created specifically to appeal to a pre-determined section of the popular music market.

In business terms it doesn't really matter which style teenagers choose – so long as they spend that pocket money! The same efficient attention to detail is employed in every other industry with a vested interest in the youth market: hi-fi equipment and electronic gadgets, magazines, clothing and even soft drinks.

Advertisers and marketers sustain a youth culture teeming with individuals with varying self-confidence deficiencies. Many people feel inadequate about themselves because they do not compare favourably with those around them, the 'beautiful' and 'super-cool' people they see in magazines and newspapers and on television.

To blame business for all of society's problems is neither fair nor true. Part of the responsibility for low self-confidence in our youth must rest with parents and teachers. Few realize what long-term harm they do when in moments of annoyance or anger they call young people stupid, irresponsible, lazy, selfish, inconsiderate, athletically inadequate or generally worthless.

Only recently I read an educational report highlighting the problem of low morale amongst British teachers. Tucked away near the end of the article was a comment from a teacher which basically said that there was no point encouraging pupils to do well, because everybody knows that with the high levels of unemployment in today's society, it would be wrong and irresponsible to unrealistically raise their expectations of future employment. This pathetic and unprofessional attitude is outrageous! It is small wonder so many individuals leave school with such a poor view of themselves.

Young people rarely receive the confidence-building encouragement they so desperately need. Consequently many teenagers grow into young adulthood with a lot of low self-worth 'baggage'. Low self-esteem is widely accepted as being largely responsible for the early dependence on alcohol and illegal drugs among many of today's youth.

Self-confidence is a fundamental ingredient for personal control, success and achievement. A lack of it has terrible, debilitating effects. A simple example comes immediately to mind: how many times have you attended a party, seen someone who you think is attractive yet been too shy to start a conversation because you have convinced yourself that he or she would not be interested in talking to you? Many men falsely believe that beautiful women are 'out of their league', so do nothing about talking to them. I have heard it said that many such women can spend an entire evening at a party without anyone speaking to them. Similarly, many women find it impossible to start conversations with men who have caught their eye. It's all down to a lack of self-confidence.

Self-confidence gives you a sense of inner calm and a feeling of overall control in life. Self-confident people accept themselves as they are and do not feel intimidated by others, nor do they let negativity get the worst of them. However, it is worth stating that being self-confident does not mean ramming your personality down the throats of everyone you meet!

For anyone who suffers from low self-esteem, the good news is that confidence can be learned. Once mastered, an individual will feel as though they are fully in charge of their life.

I've mentioned a number of external reasons why so many people suffer from low self-worth. But by far the most common source is an inner willingness to accept a second- or third-class position in life. People, if told often enough, come to believe the put-downs they receive from bosses, family and partners. They forget that no one, however 'important', has a right to make anyone else feel bad. At the same time, to a certain extent anyone who suffers such treatment is partially to blame. By allowing it to happen, they condone and perpetuate such behaviour. People tend to treat you the way *you let them*. Anyone who gets away with being rude, critical, overbearing, unreasonably demanding and insensitive to the feelings of others is not going to change unless he or she is made to realize that this behaviour is unacceptable.

However uncomfortable or frightening it may seem, anyone who is made to suffer in this way *must* do something about it. If you don't, you will never be in control of your life. Worse, you will waste your life being victimized by others. Whatever you derive from this book it will amount to very little if you allow yourself to continue a life in which your self-confidence is undermined by others.

The first step towards being treated with respect is to learn to respect yourself, and part of this is knowing how to behave *assertively*. This does not mean screaming and shouting;

assertiveness is *not* aggressiveness. Assertiveness means stating simply what you feel and think to those around you. It is about creating a 'win-win' situation – one where *your* rights and plans remain intact while you respond to the rights and requests of others, so both parties are satisfied.

Learning to be self-confident and assertive involves changing what could be deep-rooted and long-established patterns of thinking and behaviour. Making a distinct change in your behaviour will almost certainly feel uncomfortable. Anyone who tries to achieve too much too quickly is likely to suffer from disappointment and frustration.

Immediate changes to incorporate into your life should include eliminating these common non-assertive and self-destructive habits:

- Automatically saying 'sorry' when it is not really necessary/your fault (this seems to happen in Britain more than anywhere else).
- Saying 'Yes' when you would prefer to say 'No'.
- Trying to please everyone all the time.
- Putting yourself down, even if you think it is a way of conveying modesty.
- Being afraid to ask for what you want/need.
- Agreeing with people 'just for a quiet life'.
- If complimented, dismissing or deflecting it. *Never* do this. Instead, thank the individual offering the compliment: it will make him or her feel good.
- Asking for permission to express your thoughts and views.
- Expecting things to work out badly.
- Giving others permission to depress, upset, annoy, bully or frighten you.
- Sounding hesitant in the way you speak. Get rid of 'ums' and 'ers'.
- Allowing others to dominate your time.

- Accepting poor standards of professional service.
- Blaming family and friends for your present position in life.
- Hating or envying others. This only harms you.
- Criticizing others.
- Comparing yourself unfavourably to others. You are unique, therefore you cannot compare with anyone else.
- Allowing things you cannot change to dominate your life.
- Being afraid to just be yourself.

There is also a lot to be said for developing a habit of *acting* self-confident. After a while you will actually *become* more self-confident, and more assertive. It is worth pointing out that there may be many occasions when you may feel lacking in confidence but that most of the time those around you will not know this!

Richard Mortimore is a case in point. He is highly successful at staging business conferences but for years suffered from a chronic lack of self-confidence. He would cringe inside at the merest hint of being made the centre of attention. This all changed on his birthday a few years ago. His colleagues had organized a visit from a 'kissagram' as a surprise. Unknown to Richard, someone videotaped everything. The young woman read an amusing poem and then gave him a big birthday kiss. He was dying inside with embarrassment. He desperately wanted to escape. Later, when all the fuss had died down, he was shown the video. Much to his astonishment he did not look the way he had felt. At the time he was not aware of what he had said and was very surprised to see that he appeared in control, which accentuated even further the gap between what he had felt and how he appeared. He told me later that the incident had changed his life. Now that he knows he does not *look* self-conscious he no longer feels that way. He is far more relaxed and self-confident.

There are many assertiveness courses available these days. You can find them advertised in the personal classified sections of newspapers and magazines. If you want to learn to be more confident and assertive, why not take the first step by finding out more about these courses?

Everyone who learns to be more self-confident invariably receives a special bonus: enthusiasm. Enthusiastic people are the ones who actually get things done in this world. Enthusiasm is what turns any idea into reality. And enthusiasm is linked closely with happiness.

Happiness

Think back to your childhood for a moment – in particular the few weeks leading up to an especially memorable and enjoyable Christmas. Remember the excitement, the visits to the stores, the atmosphere and the general hustle and bustle. Maybe you wrote to Father Christmas asking for a bicycle, a dolls' house or a train set. Now think about that Christmas Eve, putting up your Christmas sock or stocking, possibly above the fireplace, or at the end of your bed. How much effort did your parents have in getting you off to bed? Indeed, how much trouble did you think you would have going to sleep? Christmas Day would eventually arrive. The moment you were awake (sometime between 4 and 6am if it was like my house!) you may have rushed to the pile of gifts under the Christmas tree and started ripping open your presents with total joy. You would try so hard not to make any noise because you knew that, for some reason, your parents were always particularly tired on Christmas morning.

When we grow up we tend to forget these intense feelings of joy and happiness. The closest we get may be while we make love passionately or, if we have children ourselves, watching their little faces when they open Christmas and birthday presents and re-living the moments we enjoyed so much at their age.

So what goes wrong? Why is it that life is not as happy now as it was then for millions of people? More responsibilities, stress and lack of time are certainly major contributing factors, but I believe the answer is far more basic than that. As adults we no longer have anyone to 'stage-manage' our happiness. When we were children our parents would often build up our excitement in exactly the same way as professional actors and musicians build to a climax in their performances. This does not just happen by chance: it is totally stage-managed. When it is skilfully done, by the end of an outstanding show we are on our feet cheering and applauding. Many parents do something similar with their children to build their excitement in the lead-up to special events.

I will always remember one specific birthday when I was a child. For weeks beforehand I was told by my father that my birthday present was going to be very special. Neither he nor my mother would tell me what it was, but they assured me I would absolutely love it. My mind did somersaults for weeks trying to guess what they had bought for me. It became something of a game – I would try to persuade them to tell me if my guesses were even 'warm' – they led me on, gently teasing me until, by my birthday, I could hardly contain myself.

The present certainly lived up to my expectations. It was my first *real* fishing rod and reel. Up until then I'd had a toy one – no use at all in catching the 'whoppers' I was convinced I could catch. That fishing rod was used constantly for many years and I looked after it with all the love and care in the world. (This example came to mind because just a month or so ago I was rooting through my parents' loft and there it was – a lot smaller than I remembered it, of course – but the moment I found it, my eyes glazed over as I replayed in my mind many of the fishing trips I went on in my childhood. And to think it was 'just' a fishing rod.)

Obviously, happiness does not have to be related to receiving gifts, but my aim is to illustrate how feelings of happiness can last for a long time with a little careful 'stage-management'. If my parents had not behaved in the way they did, without doubt I would still have appreciated the present but it would not have had nearly the same impact.

Today's relative affluence means that when we decide we want something, we can go out immediately to buy it. We may also find ourselves in shops where something catches our eye and then make an impulsive decision to buy it. If we do not have enough money, no problem – we are encouraged to pay by credit card, finance agreement or even with interest-free credit. Everything is geared towards speeding up the buying process. These days we are positively encouraged to be impulsive, to buy on a whim. Consequently, we now miss out on the days, weeks or months of anticipation and excitement which are so much a part of fully appreciating life's little luxuries.

I am sure you know of children who want and get the latest toys, electronic video games and gadgets from their eager-to-please parents. Many adults similarly 'spoil' themselves with grown-up toys. But once they get them, many quickly lose interest and move on to wanting something else. Immediate gratification tends to breed this apathy, a lack of appreciation and a degree of unhappiness.

These days our lives are rarely stage-managed as they were when we were children. But they could be. The secret is to build into your own life an ongoing series of stage-managed events. Plan things to look forward to. For example, if you decide to take a holiday, make a point of reading all you can about your destination and places of interest before you go. Plan a year ahead if necessary. Countless people don't bother – they say they are too busy. They miss out on so much.

There was a time, not too long ago, when workers would look forward to a solitary day each year at somewhere like Blackpool or Coney Island. Everyone would look forward to that day for months and then talk about the fantastic day they had for months afterwards. Today, with so many options to choose from throughout the entire world, we rarely get 'excited' as such.

Stage-managing your life need not concern only major events. Reward yourself for jobs well done. Tell yourself that once you have completed a particular chore you will spoil yourself by doing something special. Then make an effort to look forward to it – don't give it to yourself straight away – delay the enjoyment so that you can savour it.

If you want to be more happy in life, don't limit the stage-management of events to your own life – provide it as a service to your family and friends. Who knows? – they might do the same for you.

While on the subject of doing things for others, if you find yourself thinking about someone, don't keep it to yourself – write a note, phone or visit to let that person know he or she means something to you. If you spot something in the papers which you think may be of interest to a client or a business colleague, cut it out or copy it and send it off to him or her.

If you truly want to indulge yourself, try this: do something kind and generous for somebody else, but don't tell him or her – or any other living soul – what you have done. The warm feelings you experience when you help someone else are diluted when you try to take credit for your good deed by telling others; kept as a secret they percolate through your entire body. You know something others don't – it is a wicked pleasure.

It is important to realize that it really is OK to feel good about yourself. The more you do it, the better you can feel.

Striving for a permanent state of happiness is not only unrealistic but impossible. When we do this we are effectively chasing a 'happiness mirage': as we approach what we think is the key to complete happiness and success the 'mirage' moves off once again – far enough away to see, but not too far to make us think that pursuing it is not worthwhile. We have all said to ourselves, 'I'll be happy just as soon as I get that promotion' or 'I'll be happy just as soon as I have managed to save enough money for my dream house.' Happiness is about *now*, this second, this minute, this hour. How do you really feel about your life right now? On a scale of 1–10, what would you score? What would you expect to feel if you were to score 10 – is it realistic? If not, why not? Our expectations for happiness are often based on an idealized version of what we think others enjoy; we compare ourselves with something that does not really exist. Happiness and joy are always temporary.

Your circumstances may seem dire. Perhaps you feel you haven't much to be happy about. Try to imagine being happy at this precise moment, while you are reading this book. Tell yourself that there is nothing you would prefer to be doing with your time. Young children have the ability to become so engrossed in what they are doing that nothing else matters. We forget how to do this when we get older. We take everything far too seriously. We forget how to play. Our play becomes competitive – we need to be good, we need to win. This means it stops being play.

Happy people get totally involved in whatever they are doing. They concentrate on the process, not the result. Because the process always takes longer than the result, they feel happier for longer. Unhappy people want to be somewhere else while they are at work yet feel terribly guilty while relaxing because they feel they should be at work! They tend to feel the need to constantly chop and change their activities in much the same way as they would zap from TV channel to TV channel vainly trying to find something interesting to watch. It is highly likely that even if they find something, they will still keep zapping channels just in case something better crops up elsewhere. That is how they go through life – always on the look-out for something better. They don't know exactly what they want – just something 'better'. They insist on everything being perfect, all the time. Life is not as convenient as that – it does not make sense. Anyone who tries to make it satisfy their idealized vision will be disappointed. This can only breed ulcer-inducing stress and dissatisfaction. Such individuals rarely feel happy or satisfied with anything. They lead unfulfilled lives, always feeling that there is something missing.

It is a bit of a cliché to say that 'life is all about the journey, not the destination' but this was illustrated very well by a BBC TV producer friend of mine. Richard Rees decided to walk the entire length of the Pembrokeshire coastal path in west Wales. It is an 80-mile trip through some stunningly beautiful cliff-top scenery. I was brought up in Pembrokeshire and know the route extremely well, having walked much of it myself. He told me that it had taken him a week, he'd been exhausted and had blisters all over his feet. I tried to console him by saying that all that beautiful scenery must have made it worth it. 'I wouldn't know,' he said. 'All I saw were my feet!' Isn't that exactly how so many of us live our lives – too busy with our heads down to appreciate what's all around us?

So many experiences that should be enjoyable are allowed to become an inconvenience or a nuisance. How many times have you arranged to go to the cinema, a concert, the theatre or a dinner party with friends only to find that you are so busy with work that you have barely had time to look forward to it beforehand? On the night you have to rush madly to get there, by which time it has become more of a chore than a delight. This is what happens to the many people who fail to feel happy in spite of having all the ingredients and opportunities for a happier life.

We make all sorts of excuses for not having fun: we are too young, too old, too fat, we are afraid of looking stupid in front of our children, our parents or our colleagues. We favour what we already know; we like our 'comfort zones' – after all, stepping into the unknown is difficult. We insulate ourselves against possible discomfort, ridicule or unhappiness. The irony is that we can be made to feel unhappy simply by *not* stretching ourselves; if we don't risk anything we can suffer just as much as if we do.

I am not suggesting that you should go out of your way to experience pain or emotional turmoil, but the so-called 'Law of Reciprocity' states that you simply cannot enjoy real happiness or success if you have not experienced unhappiness or failure. It's only when we fail that we find out who and what we are.

Are you one of those people who never gets around to trying new activities? Is it because you don't think you will be any good at them? You can have so much fun once you stop caring so much about the prospect of being laughed at. Those who are willing to 'have a go' find that the only ones who laugh are those who don't get involved themselves, and they are the real losers in life.

Happy people accept what they cannot change and are happy with what and who they are. They like themselves and have learned that if they feel good about themselves just about everything around them takes on a more pleasant appearance. Isn't it strange that it is OK to tell others that you feel fed up, tired, stressed and depressed? To conform in today's society it seems that *you must look miserable and behave accordingly!*

Happy people attract friends like magnets. They know the true value of friendship and the importance of spreading happiness wherever they go. Happiness begins on the inside. Unhappy people believe (mistakenly) that happiness comes from outside. They are convinced that money, position or power equals happiness.

Tiredness is a serious problem in society. We stay up late 'enjoying ourselves' and force ourselves to get up early the next morning. Fatigue leads to unnecessary stress and irritability which makes us unhappy. Millions of people try to survive without enough sleep. Try to get into the habit of 'spoiling' yourself with a regular dosage of the right amount of sleep.

According to the World Health Organization there are an estimated 100 million people suffering from depression at any one time. There is evidence to support the idea that depression in all its different forms has increased dramatically over the last fifty years. Common sense tells us that this increase in depression *must* be related in some way to the sheer pace and complexity of life in today's society.

Of course, it can be very difficult being 'up' all the time. Everybody feels 'low' or lacking in energy at some time. You can't be bothered to do anything, you feel generally lethargic and unfulfilled. Getting out of bed can be difficult. Feeling this way is part of being alive; it is a natural state. Once we learn to understand this we are far more likely to overcome its debilitating effects quickly and make the most of being alive.

On this subject I cannot help thinking of my all-time favourite movie, *It's a Wonderful Life* (directed by Frank Capra). Just in case you don't know it, James Stewart stars as George Bailey – an ordinary guy who finds himself at his lowest ebb and on the brink of suicide. His wish that he'd never been born is granted by an obliging AS-2 (Angel Second Class). When George is shown what life is like for those living in his home-town of Bedford Falls without him, he (and we) see how one person's life touches and enriches the lives of everyone around him.

The closing shot of the film has become famous for saving the lives of viewers who were on the brink of suicide themselves. It is an inscription in a book which reads: 'Remember, no man is a failure who has friends . . .'

8

'Pick Up a Purpose'

> 'The future belongs to those who have prepared
> for it.'
> *Anon*

The best definition of a goal I have come across is: 'any
worthwhile dream with a deadline'. The problem with goals
is that, even though so many people realize how essential they
are, they are spoiled for choice and end up going through life
without a clear idea of exactly what they want to do or achieve.
In this chapter we will take a look at setting, implementing and
achieving realistic goals.

Every successful person I have met and interviewed has had
a clear set of goals; goals for the short, medium and long term.
Their lives have had a clear focus. Setting goals is about
working out priorities in your life. But where do you start?

Mission Statement

The first and most important step in setting goals and
regaining overall control in your life is to decide on a clearly
defined *purpose*. Look at any successful business organization
– it will almost certainly have a 'mission' statement: a short
sentence or two that encapsulates exactly why the company
exists. This has the effect of communicating a common
message not only to employees but to existing and potential

customers. A mission statement provides people at all levels of an organization with the opportunity to 'sing off the same hymn sheet'; it concentrates everyone's effort in a common direction.

If large and successful corporations feel the need to co-ordinate their actions for the most effective results, so should you as an individual. By focusing your time and effort into activities that satisfy a common end you will be far more likely to accomplish whatever you set out to achieve.

Many successful individuals already do this. A few years ago I had the opportunity to interview Chris Bonington, the internationally renowned mountaineer. A mutual friend had told me that Chris keeps a personal motto inside his diary which he looks at every day; my friend suggested I bring this up during the conversation. When I mentioned it Chris was amazed that I knew about it: he thought I must have researched very thoroughly for the interview! He was pleased to tell me and my radio listeners his personal 'mission' statement: 'My purpose of living is the joy of discovery, and meeting challenges, in harmony with the people around me.' He said that he had thought about that statement every day for many years. He had found himself in some very tight situations on some of his expeditions, but this affirmation had always put his life back into perspective.

Knowing Chris had a guiding principle in life gave me an insight into how he was always able to appear so calm and in control. The idea of having an overall 'purpose' in life has stayed with me ever since my meeting with him. I spent a great deal of time trying to work out something similar for myself and discovered that it was not an easy task. The complexities and sophistication of modern life seem to distance us from gaining a deeper perspective. Looking for my own purpose was a bit like digging for gold, but instead of the back-breaking, pick axe-swinging effort required for extracting the valuable ore from the ground, I was faced with something far more demanding – thinking very deeply!

I am convinced that most people don't bother spending time on themselves in this way because in the short term it is easier not to bother. We have been conditioned always to take the easy option. It is so much quicker to accept the promise that we will be happy and successful if we own the most fashionable designer dress or the latest 16-valve turbo, fuel-injected convertible. But investing time in trying to define your own purpose is the most important issue affecting your life.

I came to realize that I devoted quite a considerable amount of time presenting training videos, writing scripts and making presentations. This helped me to understand that my purpose for living was simply . . . 'to help others to help themselves'. It's funny, but since I chose this personal motto my life has become far simpler, less cluttered and more focused. It is almost as if most of what I now do fits somewhere into a bigger picture, in a deeply satisfying way. If something does not fit within the parameters I have now established, I try to weed it out of my life. The result is that I waste far less time than I used to.

Strangely enough, for quite some time I had had a nagging desire to get involved in some form of charity work. When you work in radio and television you are always being asked to lend your support to a wide variety of charitable causes. Invariably the organizers want you to help them raise money. I found I wanted to get involved more directly, in something other than fund-raising.

Almost like magic I came across a small, relatively unknown charity called TFSR (Tools for Self-Reliance). In simple terms, TFSR collect old, discarded hand tools (there are an estimated 50 million in Britain alone) and refurbish, resharpen and fit them with new handles, etc. These renewed tools are then assembled into specially designed tool kits and sent to isolated villages in countries such as Tanzania in Africa, where they are then used by local people to build their own houses and grow their own food.

Not only does TFSR help others to help themselves, but for

this aspect of their work they recycle what is regarded as 'junk' to many into items that are not only useful but actually help to save lives. Young volunteers collect the unwanted tools from people who just want to clear out their garages and lofts. The tools are then handed over to TFSR volunteers who devote their time and skill cleaning and restoring them to their former usefulness. For me, it is also important to know that no one who benefits can or will repay me for my work with TFSR. My work for this organization has helped make my life worth living.

I am explaining all this in an attempt to show you how to go about defining a purpose for yourself. Every successful corporation aims to be the best at what it does. Making money is obviously a major priority, but those businesses that realize the importance of providing excellence have discovered that making money then takes care of itself. Take a leaf out of their book.

What can you give? What will you be remembered for? Will people say that you managed to stay the distance without contributing anything to anybody else? Wouldn't that be a sad way to be remembered?

Giving yourself a clear purpose will be an invaluable help in setting and implementing your personal goals. Your purpose will be the 'hook' on which to hang everything else. So give it some careful thought, get a pen and paper, and try to come up with ways of finishing the sentence, 'My purpose in life is to . . .' If it helps, make some notes over the next few days. They could relate to how you feel about yourself, your spouse, family and friends. Think about the aspects of your work or hobbies which interest you particularly. Ask yourself why you are attracted to these people and activities. Once your notes are completed, study them to find a common thread.

Goal-setting

When you are a child, you have dreams, ambitions and hope: you want to be an adventurer, you want to make changes and improvements to the world. By the time you have grown up, you've probably been talked out of those plans – usually by people who have not achieved much themselves. When you were at school did the Careers Officer say, 'No, you can't do *that*. Do something a bit more sensible . . . there is far more security working in a bank'? Well-meaning parents similarly may have encouraged you to go into a career or profession 'with prospects' rather than something a bit more risky but, for you, infinitely more attractive. Millions of us go through life not doing the things we really *want* to as a result. Small wonder that so many of us just drift along.

Just look around the streets at the old people you see. There's no doubt that the vast majority of them have led a hard life, often without most of the luxuries we now regard as necessities. They should be able to enjoy their retirement in the twilight years of their life without the worry of not being able to pay their bills or have enough to eat. Are you going to be like that when you retire? If you say 'no', what makes you think so now? I'm sure if you'd asked them, when they were young, they'd have said 'no' too.

They were probably too busy trying to earn enough to feed and clothe their families to think about the future. Life isn't as harsh these days. Don't be like them. It's never too early to plan for the future.

Just as in football, you can't win in life if you don't score goals. No professional football player would ever go out on to the pitch saying to himself 'Oh, I'll kick the ball about a bit – maybe I will win.' He will train hard with a squad of other players and they will all be given proven strategies so that when they go on to the pitch they can all work together to score as often as they can. By working together, they all benefit.

Most people try single-handedly to take on the world, without any thought, training or planning. They don't even know where the goalposts are, so how can they possibly win? They are too busy being kicked, pushed and shoved around to think about winning or even to enjoy themselves. They do not realize that they can have as many sets of goalposts as they want, positioned wherever *they* decide – and that the ball can be changed according to their own specifications.

Anyone without goals who claims not to have time to decide on them will *never* control his or her own life. By devoting just a little time to yourself over the course of a few days you can gain a unique insight into what opportunities already exist for you. This thinking and planning time is a tiny price to pay for the potential rewards ahead.

Goals should be divided into the following categories: career, social, emotional, spiritual and health.

In the next chapter I will tell you about how my own simple organization system allows me to get more done. It revolves around buying and using a hard-cover notebook. This is what you should do. Get a notebook and use it for writing down all your goals. Turn the book around, and from the back *write down* everything you want, as well as your plans on how to achieve it all.

Directive thinking uses specific thoughts and ideas *which must be written down*; merely thinking about them won't focus your mind enough to motivate you into doing something about them. If you don't initiate change there can be no improvement.

In the middle of the first page at the back of your notebook write the following:

'From today, I want my life to run in the direction
I want it to go. I can do and have *anything* I want
out of life – if I want it enough to *actually* do
something about it.'

Then sign your name and – most importantly, date it.

On the next few pages at the back of the book list all the things that are important to you, as well as everything you've ever dreamed of. Not just those things relating to your career or your income, but to all aspects of your life. You might find it easier if you categorize the different facets of your life by devoting separate pages (or more than one for each) to, for example, your job, hobbies, health, social life and relationships. Keep adding to the list over the course of a few days as more and more things come into your mind. If you can't think of much that you want at first, you might find it helpful to think about the things you *don't* want. This will prompt you into thinking about what you *do* want.

At this stage don't worry about how crazy or impractical these wants might seem. You can put down anything you like, but whatever it is, be as specific as you can. Writing that you want 'more money' or 'promotion' is too vague. If you want more money, decide on a specific salary. If you want a holiday, visualize it – not only where you want to go but how you'll get there and where you'll stay. Taste the food and imagine the new sights and sounds you'll experience. Think about everything else you wish for in the same way. It's only by visualizing things clearly that you will be able to take the necessary steps to make them real.

Decide which goals are priorities. What do you want to do more than anything else? Then work out a time-frame: what you're going to do this week; next week; next month; by the end of six months; where you want to be in 12 months' time.

Spend time on each of your priority goals, trying to work out how you can achieve them. Write down any obstacles that might stand in your way. Write down the names of any people you know who could help you. There might be many – write them all down. Even write down the names of any people whom you may not know personally but would like to get to know so that they can help you start achieving your goals.

Remember: your goals need not be work-related. Perhaps you'd like to increase your circle of friends, or to get involved in a local social group. Do you know anyone who could introduce you to more people?

You are now starting to be constructive about achieving what you want out of life, rather than just sitting around waiting for life to happen to you. All this is going to take time, but it's time you're devoting to yourself. You deserve it.

Here are a few other suggestions you might like to consider:

- It's funny how we only think about our health after we lose it. You might like to work out a scheme whereby you cut down on some of the things you know are bad for you and even build short periods of exercise into your week.

- Relationships are often left to take care of themselves. Taking an active part in planning joint activities with your loved one brings a relationship back to life. It shows your partner how important he or she is to you.

- Don't forget to list the hobbies you've always wanted to try but have never got round to.

When you've finished your list (for now) you should be able to see on paper, possibly for the first time in your life, the real you. Once you can see yourself you will be in a better position to do something about changing and improving yourself and your circumstances.

How often have you been told – 'No, no, no. You're thinking too big'? There is nothing wrong with having big goals so long as they are not unrealistic. Big goals can be broken down into smaller ones. Achieving the small ones will help maintain your motivation as you pursue the larger one. You'll see small results as you progress towards your overall goal. Any petty or minor obstacle won't upset you because you'll see it in perspective – as merely a short-term inconvenience.

Ask yourself one more very important question: are the goals you've written down on your list the things *you* want to achieve, or are you merely going along with ambitions that have been chosen for you by teachers, parents or spouse? All too often we are told what is 'best' for us from an early age. You may have decided that it's too late to change – but who says so? It is never too late to change, although it's not always easy. I recently met a man who'd worked his way up in a large bank in the City of London. His job had everything:

responsibility, first-class world travel and a very attractive salary. But he wasn't happy. So after a lot of thought he plucked up the courage to do what he actually wanted. He resigned and bought a flower business. Not only is he happy, but his business has done extremely well, in part because he enjoys his work. He gave up a lot – probably more than most of us would, but he knew what he wanted and was willing to do something about it. It would have been so easy to have done nothing, resigned to a comfortable but unhappy life. But he didn't accept second best. Nor should you.

Very often it's a fear of the unknown that stops us making changes in our lives before we even start. This fear is very real and is experienced by most intelligent people. In some ways it is healthy: it keeps us from tackling a large goal before we have tackled some smaller ones. But sometimes it is fear which provides the excitement in the first place to motivate us to embark on a worthwhile project. In his numerous talks, mountaineer Chris Bonington draws many similarities between climbing mountains and working in business. Both involve risk-taking, setting, implementing and achieving goals, and potential disaster.

The difference is that if you make a mistake while climbing, you die.

My younger brother Glyn is an experienced high-altitude climber – as a physical training instructor he's paid to climb, and he also goes on expeditions when he's not working. In the last couple of years he has successfully reached the summit of Mount McKinley, the highest mountain in Alaska, and more recently Annapurna 4 in the Himalayas. Within 12 hours of his team finishing their climb of Mount McKinley, three climbers from a simultaneous expedition had been killed on the mountain.

The 9-man, 3-woman joint services expedition to Annapurna 4 (summit = 24,688 ft/7,525 m) provided a dramatic example of what individuals can achieve by setting goals and carrying them through to completion.

The expedition's initial goal was to climb a Himalayan peak without using bottled oxygen or high-altitude Sherpas (native Tibetan guides). There followed a year of planning, co-ordinating and purchasing enough equipment and supplies to keep 170 porters weighed down with packs weighing approximately 9 stone/60 k each. The three-month expedition involved a 70-mile, 5-day walk just to get to the foot of the mountain.

They set off from basecamp at 12,000 ft (3,658 m) without Sherpas. The expedition went well. Glyn was one of those who reached the summit, but on the way down things became almost too difficult to cope with. Temperatures of -30°C and bitingly cold winds of 100 miles per hour added to the effects of altitude sickness. The human body starts to shut down at heights above 20,000 ft (6,100 m) where lack of oxygen, sleep and food take their toll. Seventy per cent of high-altitude climbers die while climbing – of these, a minority die from falling off mountains or being hit by an avalanche; most die after they are forced to give up through psychological and physical stress.

Glyn had lost nearly 30 lb/6 kilos in weight and had been unable to sleep properly for nearly three weeks. He couldn't eat for four days as his stomach had ceased working. His body and mind then gave in to the mountain. He was incapable of going any further. He stopped his descent and allowed himself to go to sleep, knowing he would never wake up again.

His climbing partner saved his life by waking him up and forcing him to continue. The next day Glyn's partner gave up in the same way. It was then Glyn's turn to save a life. Eventually all the climbers reached basecamp successfully. All had suffered severe frostbite; one of them had to spend six days in hospital at Katmandu suffering from dehydration. Another climber fell victim to severe mountain sickness.

It is so easy to dismiss such achievements by saying 'Well, why on earth put yourself in such a position?' But, as Glyn says, 'Life just gives you time and space, it's up to us as individuals to fill it with as much as possible before we die. So many people live for 80 or 90 years but do nothing with it. Climbing mountains provides me with the ultimate physical and mental challenge. One day I will die anyway, so I want to pack as much in as possible. A lot of people think that climbers have a death wish – that's not true. We do everything we can to stop dying.'

I'm incredibly proud of him. Such a climb is a huge achievement in itself, but particularly so for Glyn, who wasn't allowed to take part in any sport when he was younger because he suffered from a condition called Osgood-Schlatter disease. Doctors agreed that taking part in any strenuous sport could seriously harm him.

Any goal can be as challenging, terrifying and rewarding as Glyn's, if you really want it. Goals nearly always involve fear of the unknown. Their goal to climb Annapurna 4 could quite easily have been carrying out any other satisfying projects, not necessarily physically dangerous ones. For example, it could have been a plan to start a new business or build a dream house.

Once you've made a commitment to yourself for whatever you plan to do, realize there will definitely be problems along the way. But because you will know where you are going you will be able to keep everything in perspective. It's the way that people overcome problems that often makes the difference between success and failure. Indeed, without solving such problems you would miss out on any feelings of achievement – which is what makes things worth while in the first place.

As for my brother's climbs, I'm sure there have been times when he's been scared and said to himself, 'What the hell am I doing here?' (or words to that effect!). But he kept going. And that's the point. Successful people don't let fear get in their way.

I will never forget spending a day with my brother and a small group of Gurkha soldiers in Scandinavia. As everyone took his turn climbing a 40-ft frozen waterfall in the bright winter sunshine I was quite happy merely watching and taking photographs. Then Glyn handed me 2 ice axes and a set of spiked 'crampon' boots. He told me I was going to climb the waterfall – I won't tell you what *I* said to him! Suffice to say he persuaded me to give it a try. Slowly and very nervously I inched my way up the vertical sheet of ice, digging my spikes and axes in as deeply as I could! Eventually I reached the top, to applause from the rest of the climbers.

I would never have believed I could do such a climb. It goes to show how our ability is so often far greater than we think. With expert help and guidance I was able to achieve something I would never have attempted otherwise. I was quite happy being a spectator, but once I got involved – I was as high as a kite for days afterwards.

Successful people are individualists. They don't mind being different. They don't mind standing out from the crowd. So be different, be better than the crowd. Take a few chances: have a little bit more fun than the rest. Set priorities in your life. By asking yourself what obstacles stand in your way you can then analyse what can be done about overcoming them. Most important of all, *initiate change*. This is the crux of being truly successful. You have to initiate change for yourself. Millions wait – and wait and wait – and nothing ever happens.

So do something – anything – to change your life. It does not matter how small a change you make. Remember, if you don't do anything now, today, this week, you will find that one day in the future you will look back and say 'Oh, I wish I had.' *Do something new and different*, today.

Read your list of goals every day and think about them to ensure they become firmly crystallized in your mind. By reinforcing them in this way they will become a part of you. It's so important to keep your eye on the big picture. Visualize the way you want to be in one, five or even ten years' time. When you've decided on your goals, set yourself realistic deadlines, breaking the time-span down in such a way that you know where you want to be on any project at any given time. Then you'll have something to work for. If you find that your deadlines are unrealistic, reschedule them. But whatever you do, don't give up!

Being successful is not only knowing what you want, but preparing yourself for getting it. Know deep in your subconscious that you *are* going to get there. This will be conveyed through your attitude to build quiet self-confidence. Fill your thoughts with what you have already accomplished and build on those achievements. If necessary write them down, too, it's a wonderful builder of self-confidence.

Some worthwhile goals can take years to achieve. If you decide to become a doctor it might take seven years. Anybody who thinks he or she will need one year to achieve such a goal is obviously going to fail. But this is not a failure, simply an unrealistic goal.

Remember, you *must* write down your goals if you want to initiate any meaningful improvement in your life. It is *that* important.

Before we leave the subject of goals, why not select three, four or five minor goals you can work on every day? They could be anything: reading a chapter from a book, decorating a room where you live, learning to play a musical instrument or to paint or sketch. Imagine, in six months' time, what you will have achieved simply because you made a conscious decision today to allocate a small amount of time each day towards accomplishing what, by your own admission, you have decided you want to achieve in life.

Now the important part – how do you turn your goals and ambitions into reality? You can have all the best intentions, but nothing will ever happen until *you* do something about them! If you wait for something to happen all you will succeed at is getting old, grey or bald and probably very frustrated. If you want to achieve anything you have to start *now*. Not tomorrow, next week, next month or at any other time. Those who say 'I'll get round to it' never do. For anything to be effective it has to start now.

9

Time-Management and Organization

We are distracted through our newspapers and magazines, on television and the radio, billboards, posters and brochures. It gets on our clothes and it even comes through our mail box. These constant demands on our time, however, provide us with fewer moments to think about our own well-being, our future and what is important to us.

The most effective persuaders will win you as their prize – that is, until someone else comes along seconds, minutes or hours later to drag you away to something else which they will promise is even more interesting or appealing. We are drowning in demands on our time. The busier we become, the more we are forced to endure. The saying is 'Time is money.' It is more fundamental than that: 'Time is LIFE.' It is our most precious commodity. Everything can be quantified by time. Indeed, the fast-food giant McDonalds has devised its own 'international time currency': prices for their products are gauged according to the number of minutes an average consumer would have to work to earn enough to pay for a 'Big Mac'!

The only answer is effective time-management and organization. Time is finite: no matter how young, old, rich, poor, intelligent or otherwise, everyone gets the same 24 hours in a day and 168 hours in a week. You can't stop time, save it or accrue interest on it.

So much has been written about time-management that it

would probably take weeks to read it all. Companies have sprung up all over the world offering seminars on their own unique time-management techniques. Their systems usually involve purchasing 'luxurious' and often expensive 'time-planning' diaries and so forth. No doubt some of these services are valuable, but it seems to me that many are a waste of money and of the time they are meant to save you.

Let me start by quoting Mark McCormack, Chief Executive of the sports-management company IMG. Mark is well known for his devotion to time-management. He says, 'Mastering time is to do the things *you* planned on doing, *when* you planned on doing them, and for *no longer* than you planned.'

A simple and effective philosophy, but how to put it into practice? There is one essential element needed before it can work: planning. You cannot use your time effectively if you do not consistently plan the way you are going to spend it. (This does *not* have to mean pre-determining everything you do, at all times. Let's be realistic here!) So often we stumble from one deadline to another, merely trying to cope with the demands others make on our time. We can easily find ourselves bogged down by relatively insignificant matters.

Your time is the commodity everybody wants from you. As discussed in previous chapters, businesses spend large sums of money to attract and if possible, hold your attention. The effect of these and all other unsolicited intrusions into your life is less time to spend on yourself and your future well-being.

We are luckier than many of our ancestors in that we now have a multitude of ways to spend time. Working hours are shorter, holidays are longer and we get them more often. Another case of 'We've never had it so good'.

It's surprising, therefore, how little time people devote to their own development and growth. They don't invest in their own future. They say, 'I haven't got time – I'm too busy.' What they actually mean is they are too involved in doing for others; they cannot see the importance of dedicating a little time every day towards pursuing some of their own goals in life.

You have a choice: you can react to what's going on around you or influence it. You can take control for yourself or you can submissively let others (family, friends, work colleagues or business clients) dictate what you do and when. Obviously some of your time will have to be spent responding to the demands of others; but if you are doing this for most of the time you will *never* reach any of the goals you have set for yourself.

To make the most of your time you must:

- be aware of how you spend your time;

- eliminate any time-wasting tasks and, if possible, the people who consistently waste your time;

- find ways to get things done a bit quicker;

- extend your day: get up earlier if necessary; and

- learn to be more organized in your daily life.

The most successful people in the world don't get any more time in a day than you or me, so it must be a case of 'It's not what they've got, but what they do with it.' People who use time effectively have made a fundamental decision: *they* dictate the terms of how they spend it. They know how to set priorities, plan ahead and follow through with everything they decide is important. Being disorganized is a massive and needless waste of time. Indeed, organized people will tell you that it makes life far easier.

For the purposes of gaining control in your life there are basically two types of activity that use up your time – *Catching-up* jobs and *Getting-ahead* jobs.

Catching-up jobs include mundane chores, correspondence and all those other tasks we would never do if given the choice. *Getting-ahead* tasks involve anything to help you improve yourself – your education, health, career and your emotional and spiritual life.

Simply by increasing the number of *Getting-ahead* jobs

you do, you will increase dramatically your future chances of success. Add to this a reappraisal of your *Catching-up* tasks, eliminate as many of them as you can – and you will see immediate improvements in your use of time – this is guaranteed!

It is a sad fact of human nature that, when an individual's schedule becomes 'too full', personal goals and priorities are often the first to be put off to some undefined time in the future. *Getting-ahead* goals should never be relegated in favour of *Catching-up* tasks. If you want maximum control of your time you must strike a balance between the two.

Write It Down

The first step towards getting more done in less time is to get into the habit of *writing down* everything you ever want or need to do. If you do not already keep a daily 'to do' list, this is the time to start. You cannot hope to be in control without being able to see at a glance what needs to be done. Trying to keep such information in your head is a waste of mental ability. Once something is committed to paper it is far more likely to be completed. What is more, you get a wonderful sense of satisfaction and accomplishment when you can cross tasks off your list once they have been completed.

To make the most of your time and to be organized involves developing some form of personal system. No individual system is better than any other, it is simply down to your own choice. You *must* find something that works for you. As someone who hates paperwork with a vengeance I have developed a system which is as simple as possible. Maybe it will be a help to you.

I have a fairly thick, ruled notebook (as opposed to a note-pad), about twice the size of this paperback book. My whole life revolves around this book – everything (*except* diary information) goes into it. I scribble in it, jot down phone numbers, write notes when I am attending meetings and list everything I need to do. This book has become well worn and well travelled – but I know that everything I have done is in that book. As no one else needs to see it the notes can be (and often are) as messy as I please. Needless to say, as something so important in my life, it is never out of my sight.

I have given myself a number of rules relating to this book. For instance, I have banned writing notes on isolated scraps of paper! If unavoidable, I will stick the note inside my notebook as it is, rather than waste time rewriting it in the book itself.

On the left side of each double-page spread I write my 'to do' lists, which I usually date at the top. All items on these pages are given a small left-hand margin so that as each item has been completed I can tick it off. It is then easy to see at a glance which items are still outstanding. I try to make of point of dating my 'to do' lists as this helps me find any notes that relate to particular projects I am involved in. I make no attempt to write tidily or to ensure that every page is written on – some look like battlegrounds littered with dead doodles!

At the back of the notebook, I list my short-, medium- and long-term goals, personal priorities and any other promises to myself. This way I can keep them in my mind by looking at them on a regular basis.

My notebook goes everywhere with me. It is in constant use. Whenever I have a few spare moments I flick through the 'to do' pages, reminding myself of what needs to be done and ticking off those tasks I have completed, crossing out tasks I have decided not to do and adding anything new. I find myself continually wanting to do something – anything, to get an item or two 'ticked off'.

By ensuring that everything goes into the book, I know immediately where everything is! Every couple of months or so I go through the book and use a coloured marker to highlight every name, address and telephone number. I then transfer these *en masse* into my computer 'database'. The database is then sorted and printed up as my latest address book. This way, I rarely lose phone numbers or addresses.

Give this simple system a try, it might work for you. If you are not yet in the habit of writing 'to do' lists – please start. It quickly becomes a good habit and once something is written down it takes on a tangible quality – looking through my older notebooks I can see how productive I have been, which has the effect of encouraging me to get even more done.

Write down *every* task that needs doing: social, family and professional obligations. Once you have written everything down, go back over your list item by item. Learn to notice which tasks are *Catching-up* and which ones are *Getting-ahead*. For every item, ask yourself what would be the worst thing that could happen if you decided *not* to do it. It may be that by ignoring a few of the tasks you can save yourself a great deal of time.

Next, ask yourself which of the remaining tasks you could delegate to someone else. The aim is to free up as much of your time as possible for your *Getting-ahead* projects. With a little careful planning you should find you are able to start on personal projects which up until now you have never felt capable of beginning. Remember: the more *Getting-ahead* tasks you complete, the more productive you will become.

Those who work 16 hours a day, every day, thinking it's the way to get on, are deluding themselves by confusing activity with achievement. Remaining busy generates nothing except stress and/or chronic fatigue. There is a huge difference between working *hard* and working *smart*. Everyone needs to be able to sit back from his or her situation and evaluate whether time is being spent in the most efficient and productive way.

Procrastination is also a serious form of 'achievement constipation'. Filling time with low-priority work is easily done and is often a form of procrastination – delaying the start or completion of an unpleasant or daunting task. There are a number of remedies: you can identify the unpleasant task and then try to decide on its smallest and least daunting aspect. Give yourself a maximum of five minutes to work on this aspect of the task. You might find that, once you have got started, it will be much easier to continue.

When you survey your list of tasks, notice which ones are the most difficult. Start with them first. Once they are completed you will experience the enormous satisfaction of knowing that the rest of your tasks will be easy by comparison.

Given the chance, most people will readily try to off-load jobs on the first available person who'll agree to do them. They take advantage of the fact that most of us have difficulty saying 'No'. It's so easy – whether at work or socially – to find yourself snowed under with projects, jobs and chores you'd never *choose* to do. Don't be afraid to say 'No' firmly and politely, if you feel that a task will impinge too much on your precious time.

Here are a few points to remember about time:

- You have far more control over your time than you may think.
- Misusing time is merely a poor habit – it can be changed.
- Learn to think about *your* time. How do you spend it?
- Accept that you will always be able to find the time to do those things that mean the most to you. Many of the tasks you don't seem to get around to are probably not *that* important.

Using time efficiently involves thinking ahead. One good way to save time is to do things when others are not. For example, 44 per cent of all shoppers go to the supermarkets on a Friday or Saturday – and then complain about getting caught up in all those queues! This waste of time can be avoided simply by going shopping at a quieter time if you can. Similarly, time wasted waiting at the bank or post office can be saved if you go at a time when you know few others will be there.

If you must see your doctor or dentist, anticipate the time you'll have to spend in the waiting room. Take reading or writing material with you rather than merely killing time reading the ancient magazines on offer. Likewise, if you are going on a long journey don't read newspapers and magazines just to pass the time. Millions of commuters travel to and from work on buses and trains everyday, often reading a newspaper. Many of them are more concerned with finding a way to pass the time than with discovering what is happening in the news. Think about all this time you spend every week of your working life: imagine what you could achieve with some planning and a bit of thought! You could study any of the numerous distance learning programmes now available on cassette. These include language courses, 'talking books' and business training of all types. Use the time to write your 'to do' lists, clarify your thinking as you write down your goals, read travel books relating to future holiday destinations, inspirational, motivational and biographical books of people you admire and aim to emulate. All of these activities will help you far more than frittering away this time listening to music or reading a trashy novel!

Make a point of allocating time every day to think about, set and write down tasks and priorities. Try getting up just 15 minutes earlier in the morning, or how about grabbing some time before you leave for work or just before you go to bed? This way, your tasks for the next day will then be ready and waiting for you when you wake up.

The Pareto Principle states that 80 per cent of results are derived from only 20 per cent of one's time and effort. Learn to identify (and then eliminate or minimize) those activities that take up 80 per cent of your time but yield a return of only 20 per cent.

Here is a list of the top 10 time-wasters; avoid them whenever you can:

1. Perfectionism – trying to get things absolutely right when it is not really that important.
2. 'Doing lunch'. Admittedly this is sometimes unavoidable

for business, but it wastes hours of the working day. It can also be bad for your waistline and can cause afternoon lethargy, especially if there was alcohol on the menu.

3. Commuting to and from work at the same time as everyone else. Travel earlier or later to save time.
4. Failure to delegate.
5. People who consistently waste your time. Weed them out of your life if possible – politely re-educate those who cannot be ignored.
6. Watching television just because it is 'on'.
7. Concerning yourself with 'busy' work rather than 'productive' work.
8. Allowing interruptions to wreak havoc with your plans.
9. Worrying. It never improves a situation and often only makes things worse.
10. The telephone. A wonderful invention but all too often it is allowed to dominate our lives both at work and at home.

From this list, two items deserve special attention.

Interruptions How many times have you been in the middle of something that demanded your undivided attention only to be interrupted? Interruptions are part of everyone's life, especially for parents of young children, but anyone who allows interruptions to govern his or her life is asking for trouble. If you have *Getting-ahead* projects, it is absolutely essential to build at least half an hour of uninterrupted time into every day of your life. If this means getting up before the rest of your household or going to bed after everyone else, then this is what you must do.

By the very nature of many of our jobs, dealing with interruptions is what we are paid for. By exerting some gentle control over your working environment, however, it is often possible to build into your working day at least half an hour of time to get on with important projects. If you fail to set aside this time deliberately, projects have a habit of not getting completed – or worse, of not being started. There are obviously many exceptions to this, but most interruptions occur because one person believes his or her time is more important than anyone else's.

The Telephone For many of us, the telephone plays a major part in our working lives. However, we are often slaves to its demands: everything stops when the phone rings! At other times, no matter how hard we try, we cannot get off the phone. It is so easy to chat aimlessly, wasting valuable time. To gain control over the use of the telephone in your life, here are a few suggestions. (This is assuming, of course, that you are not a professional telephonist!)

- If possible, try to arrange your day so that there is a period which is 'phone-free' – those you speak with on a regular basis will get to know not to call at that time.
- If you haven't someone to answer the phone for you, install an answering machine. Your message should assure the caller that you will call him or her back as soon as possible. Many answer machines allow you to hear incoming messages as they are being recorded. If a call sounds particularly important you can pick up immediately and deal with it (or ring the person straight back if you don't want to give away that fact that you are, in fact, there). The sooner you realize that it is quite acceptable *not* to answer the phone just because someone wants to talk to you, the sooner you will gain more control in your life. By learning to use the phone for *your* convenience you will fundamentally improve the way you work. So many people fail to realize how the phone dominates their lives, so it is quite easy to subtly ensure that you 'call the shots'.
- Before each call, write down one-word reminders of points you want to raise during the conversation. This will focus your mind and avoid wasted time.

- I have found it particularly useful to go through my entire list of 'calls to be made' at a pre-determined time. Each day I save all my non-urgent calls for this time and make each one straight after the next. Because I know there are more calls to make, each one has to be short and to the point. It can even become a bit of fun trying to get through as many calls as possible in the shortest time. If someone starts to ramble, I can then honestly say that I have to make another call, adding that we will have to carry on our conversation at a later stage.

- If you anticipate beforehand that some calls will have to be long, schedule them near the end of the time period you have set aside. This way you ensure that all your other calls are not left outstanding if the longer calls take even more time than you envisaged.

- If you cannot get hold of someone, don't leave a message asking him or her to call you back. Give a precise time when *you* will call again – something like 3.25 p.m. rather than 'around 3.30-ish'. Be precise about scheduling your calls. Then make sure you call at the exact time you have promised.

By minimizing your telephone use, you will increase your productivity and efficiency – and free up more of your time for *Getting-ahead* tasks.

Organization

Learning to become better organized will save you countless hours. It will also reduce the amounts of stress and anxiety in your life. Being organized has a most calming effect on one's life. In contrast, a disorganized person is forced to spend their life rushing around trying to cope.

Organization basically boils down to just one concept: learning to think ahead to anticipate problems and delays. Being aware of the areas of chaos in your life can be rather depressing, but by taking small steps towards being organized you will quickly find that life becomes far easier. This in turn will motivate you to apply organization to more areas of your life.

A word of warning: you can fall into the trap of being *too* well organized. Being organized is supposed to make your life easier, not take it over. I know someone who is frighteningly well organized. Everything she does is done with military precision. She is the first to tell everyone how incredibly organized she is. She even keeps a record of her room and window dimensions with her at all times (keyed into her sophisticated electronic organizer) so that she can check immediately if an item of furniture she may want to buy will fit into her home. Yes, this is a good idea, and her organization is admirable – but she takes it to obsessive levels.

For example, she is proud of the fact that she *never* misses sending people birthday and anniversary cards. She buys greetings cards in bulk, so always has them in stock. She knows that if you want to make someone feel special – send them a card. But by telling them exactly how she never forgets she has reduced what is intended as a thoughtful and considerate gesture to an automatic, computerized process.

We marvel at the skill of stage magicians and illusionists. If they tell us how they do it we are not so impressed. This woman would be far better off if she kept her methods a secret. Don't spoil the magic; become organized but don't tell anyone how you've managed it.

Whatever you decide to do to improve your organizational ability, you will have to implement a number of systems – the simpler they are the more likely you will stick to them. You might find the following suggestions useful:

- Keep only one diary for all of your personal appointments. If your family is particularly busy keep an additional 'family' diary in the kitchen.
- Stop watching television in 'real' time – record programmes

to watch later on, at your convenience. This eliminates watching TV 'just because it is on'. If you have not watched a programme after a week goes by, ask yourself whether you really want to watch it that much – if not, record over it.

These are just two ideas; you will think of many more for yourself just as soon as you decide to take control of the way you spend your time.

10

Your Guide to Self-Marketing

Having total control of your life is obviously impossible: outside pressures and responsibilities from employers, clients, family and friends make sure of that. But you can exert far more influence and control than you may realize. In this final chapter we will look at how to apply to our own advantage many of the persuasion techniques discussed in earlier chapters to affect the way we are perceived by others.

Professional manipulators learned a long time ago that we are what we are *perceived* to be, not what we think we are. This realization and the amount of money to be earned from it has led to the massive growth of the public relations industry, which actively creates positive images for all kinds of public figures. These days politicians, professional businesspeople and the stars of sport, film, television and pop music avail themselves of publicists' expertise. Images are developed deliberately and nurtured carefully.

The career of movie-star Arnold Schwarzenegger is widely regarded as 'textbook self-marketing'. From humble beginnings he made a name for himself in his native Austria as a bodybuilder before moving to the US, a larger market where he was able to raise his profile even further. Once he reached the pinnacle of his bodybuilding career (winning the Mr Universe title), he made the most of it by securing lead roles in films such as *Conan the Barbarian* and *The Terminator*. Over the years he has consolidated his position and reached an even wider audience by developing another, more lovable public image in movies such as *Twins* and *Kindergarten Cop*. This professional success and 'box office' appeal has made him one of the most powerful performers in Hollywood.

His much-publicized marriage to Maria Shriver, a member of the famed Kennedy clan, has given him access to American politics. Who knows what else he wants to achieve? It's probably fair to say that whatever it is, he has certainly built a solid foundation for it. Not bad for someone who was told that he'd never make it because no one could pronounce his name!

Self-marketing is all about identifying, anticipating, supplying and ultimately satisfying the needs of decision-makers and those who are interested in the product or service you can provide.

Try, for a moment, to think of yourself as a product in a supermarket. You will quickly realize that there are a number of simple options open to you. You can sit there quietly and anonymously tucked away at the back of the bottom shelf waiting for someone to notice you – or you can choose to position yourself at eye level in front of those people who may want to buy you.

Selling yourself in much the same way as a professional marketer would sell a packet of washing powder is not as outlandish as it might seem. There are many similarities. To sell any product it is essential that it is displayed in its most desirable light in front of those most likely to be interested in it, at the price specified. Positioning on the shelf is therefore very important. You won't be alone on that shelf – millions of others will be jockeying for position and ultimately for the attention of employers, friends or potential partners. Because of this intense level of competition, companies invest enormous amounts of time and money ensuring that a product's image and packaging will 'flag-wave' to attract enough attention to stop a prospective consumer so that he or she takes a closer look. This must happen before anyone makes any sort of commitment to buy. The experts also know that if they put the product under the noses of enough potential buyers, statistically they have a much greater chance of selling it.

The same is true for individuals. A company that left this process to chance would soon go out of business. But countless individuals don't realize the opportunities they are missing simply by not being in control of this area of their lives. Understanding the way you are perceived by others can make a staggering difference to your lifestyle: this knowledge can bring you more respect, power, friends and a significantly higher income. When others perceive you as successful, self-assured and firmly in control of your life, it is far easier to influence them.

So what 'vibes' do you give out to others? If you can persuade others to perceive you as someone who is special, you will be treated better, your opinions will be sought more often and you will increase your perceived value. It is a common mistake for people to think that financial success is based on expertise and qualifications. Employers and customers are prepared to pay more for something they *believe* is worth more. It is also a common myth that successful people are more intelligent and better educated than the less successful. All too often, successful people are just more effective at positioning themselves and persuading others to give them the opportunity to 'shine'. Then, when they are seen to be doing well, they use each new opportunity as it arises to progress even further. You can do the same.

Think back to Arnold Schwarzenegger. I'm sure he does not consider himself the best actor in the world. His ability to command enormous fees for the movies he appears in is based on other factors such as his popularity and his way of attracting business – what is known in the trade as 'putting bums on seats'.

The Image

The first step to successful self-marketing is to list *all* your strengths and weaknesses. Your strengths might include:

- reliability
- honesty
- integrity
- particular skills and qualifications
- working well as part of a team
- being good at thinking up realistic ideas.

Weaknesses could include:

- poor attention to detail
- being too meticulous
- a habit of criticizing others
- being too confident or not confident enough
- interrupting people
- lack of specific qualifications or experience.

This information will help you to concentrate on your strengths in the future and give you a clear and realistic understanding of your own potential and limits. If you discover a number of negative aspects of your personality, appearance or behaviour, at least you will know about them and, if you choose to, will be able to do something about changing them.

Look at yourself as if you were a product. Take a long hard look and ask, 'Do I like what I see?' If you do – I suggest you look again! Be a bit critical and try to assess what other people would notice about you if they were meeting you for the first time.

In the context of self-marketing it is important to remember that regardless of what you think of yourself, everyone you meet will respond to you, whether positively, negatively or with disinterest. If you want to persuade or influence the behaviour of anyone, you must control the way they perceive you. If someone thinks you behave nervously, for example, it is irrelevant that you don't agree. It's how *they* perceive you that matters, not what you think.

An impartial appraisal is needed, so conduct a bit of 'market research' by asking trustworthy friends and family to tell you what they notice about you – good and bad! It is easy to dismiss what you don't want to hear. But if you are told the same things by different people, don't ignore them.

Write down everything. Such notes will provide you with a unique insight into the real you – as seen through the eyes of those closest to you. Be methodical in your approach – if it helps, start at the top and work down to your feet.

Here are a few points to consider:

- Do you need a haircut – or better still, would your hair benefit from a bit of styling? Visit the hairdresser regularly; don't wait until it is absolutely necessary.

- It is quite common for women of all ages to apply exactly the same type (and amount) of make-up they used when they were teenagers. Do you use too much, or maybe not enough? Get professional advice if necessary.

- How do you stand? When I originally did this self-analysis exercise my partner told me that I had a habit of not standing up straight. I didn't believe her (or probably didn't want to) so I asked a few friends what they thought – and they agreed with her! It certainly shed a different light on the other things she had told me!

- How about the way you sit? No one likes to see someone who slouches.

- Take a critical look at the clothes you wear. I will always remember interviewing someone about his new and 'innovative' book. I couldn't keep my eyes off his threadbare shirt collar and cuffs. I had noticed his shoes were rather down-at-the-heel too. He carried his papers in a rather well-worn polythene supermarket carrier bag. As a direct result of this, I couldn't help mentally questioning the value of what he had to say.

- Think about the way you talk. Do you speak clearly? Do you talk too much? Or maybe not enough?
- How about your weight? Are you fit?

Pay particular attention to how your clothes fit you. These are the most common problems: waists that are too tight, trouser legs that are too short, jacket sleeves that are too short or too tight across the shoulders, a jacket front stretched across a bulging stomach. A small, carefully selected collection of well-fitting clothes are an investment in your future. By making the best of yourself you will not only look more elegant, successful and distinguished but will feel good and more self-confident.

I am not suggesting that you rush out to the shops and buy all the latest fashions. As mentioned in earlier chapters, only commercial interests dictate fashion. What I *am* suggesting is that you develop a personal sense of style which will in turn make a positive contribution towards the way others perceive you. By appearing 'in control' you will be treated as though you are.

It's no longer good enough to be merely clean and reasonably presentable. Invest time and effort in yourself and it will pay off. Employers and clients associate high personal standards with high business standards. Put yourself in their place. Look at yourself from their point of view. People want to deal with individuals who are elegant, smart and well groomed. These days it simply isn't enough to be good at your job. The way you look and behave have become crucial parts of the job. The signals you send out to others will be judged by everyone you meet. One or two shortcomings may not spoil a generally good impression, but an overall sloppy look will.

I was once asked to advise a man in his early fifties about his severe professional problems. He was extremely handsome, with immaculate silver hair, a chiselled jaw, a deep tan and blue-grey eyes. He looked like a highly successful chief executive. But all of these positive attributes were eroded during the first few minutes of meeting him. Shaking his hand was like holding a wet, limp fish. Both his shirt cuffs were slightly frayed. His blazer was probably 25 years old. He was proud of the fact that he could still fit into the trousers he was wearing, which he had bought 20 years before. The trouble was they were slightly too short, revealing his white socks emerging from vinyl shoes.

OK, looks aren't everything, but he was also soft-spoken, apologetic, nervous and lacking in self-confidence. The combination of the clothes he wore and his behaviour had a very damaging effect on all the good Nature had blessed him with. When I told him what signals he was giving out, he found that with a bit of practice he was able to start behaving in a way that reinforced his positive attributes. In so doing he actually became more distinguished, authoritative and confident.

Not everyone is naturally good-looking, but with just a bit of thought and attention to detail you too can help transform yourself. The change may not be radical but it could make a difference. This difference, however small, could be all that is keeping you from winning that promotion, new contract or the heart of someone you find attractive.

Systematically creating a positive image will provide you with more opportunities in all areas of your life. You will increase the esteem in which others hold you. This in turn will provide you with even more opportunities. This will become an ongoing process.

The more you are seen to be in demand, the more people will want you. Film and television stars have known this for years. Obviously we can't all be stars, but there is no reason why you can't be seen as one within your own circle of activity.

Your self-image is too important for your future success to

allow it to take care of itself. In a fair world it would not be necessary to consider how you are perceived, but unfortunately we don't live in such a world.

Just the Job

If you still need convincing, let me use the example of 'getting a job' – and not just any job: the best job you could ever dream of (why aim low?) You will see how effective self-marketing can make a difference to the outcome.

You have seen an advertisement for *the* job. It is genuinely perfect for you, calling for the qualifications, expertise and experience you already have. In return the job has *everything* you could possibly want. The only thing missing from the actual advertisement is a headline mentioning you by name and pleading with you to take the job!

What happens? You write a letter, send off your application and wait for a response. You may then find that either you don't get an interview or, if you do, that the job is given to someone else, someone you feel certain is not the best person for the job. As you know, this can and does happen regularly. Employers often recruit the wrong people. They don't want to, but I'm sure you know of many occasions on which people seem to get promoted to their level of ineptitude.

When you don't get the 'perfect' job it is easy to put it down to favouritism, nepotism, a personality clash or plain bad luck. You probably feel initial disappointment and then try to rationalize the situation by telling yourself 'it wasn't to be'.

The truth can be devastatingly simple and rather brutal. It is highly likely that you lacked the necessary *control* over the way you were perceived by the decision-maker. The presentation and content of your application letter and résumé must have failed to convey how good you really are, or perhaps when you met the employer the signals you sent were not those received.

Obviously no one can ever be guaranteed success when

applying for a job, but you can certainly shift the odds in your favour. The techniques that follow are proven strategies that I have developed in conjunction with Coutts Career Consultants Ltd, Great Britain's largest career counsellors.

The Résumé The good news is that when you apply for a superb job you are invariably competing with a lot of people who have submitted low-grade applications. The bad news is – yours could be low-grade, too!

People who are unskilled at self-marketing often have totally unrealistic ideas about how to apply for a job. Being offered a worthwhile job is akin to running in a high-level athletics meeting. Without preparation, the right training and a winning approach to the task you will get beaten at the tape. A docile approach rarely gets the desired result.

First, contrary to what most people think, a written job application rarely gets you a job – only an interview. Therefore it is essential that your letter and résumé persuade the prospective employer to want to meet you. When large quantities of applications arrive they are usually sorted into three piles: 'A's – definite interview material; 'B's – maybes; and 'C's – rejections. So your first persuasion task is to make sure you get into the 'A' pile – or at the very least the 'B' pile. If you go into the 'C's – you are dead!

Employers advertising a job are telling you that they have a need – it is up to you to coax them into believing that only you can fulfil this need. Don't take what they state in the advertisement too literally. If you really want the job, set about manipulating them into seeing you as the best possible candidate and making you an offer. For instance, if they specify a particular age bracket and you don't satisfy this – still apply.

Most people who write job application letters merely ask to be considered for the job. Asking for something always puts you in a weak position. Offer something strong and relevant in your letter and you will begin to affect the decision-makers' perception of you in a positive way. Help them to solve their problem. Look at the situation from their point of view – not yours. Why are you worth seeing? What have you got to offer? How can you help them? If you cannot answer these questions, you certainly cannot expect a potential employer to do so.

I have seen countless applications handwritten on paper that has been ripped out of cheap notepads. Usually these are immediately put into pile 'D': the rubbish bin. Your overall presentation must be immaculate if you are to reach the next stage.

Your accompanying CV or résumé will be scanned for up to 20 or 30 seconds. If the reader does not find what he or she is looking for, it (and you) will be discarded. The style, layout, content and running order of most résumés are the same. They often share one overriding similarity – they're boring! A résumé that gets results is far more than just a list of your qualifications and achievements. It should persuade the reader to believe that you are worth meeting. It should hint at a lively, interesting personality – someone who would make a valuable contribution to the company in question.

Your résumé should be thought of as a personal advertisement – not merely a list of facts and dates. The secret is to include something that will intrigue the reader. Try to humanize yourself – you will appear more interesting. But don't try too hard! One example comes to mind. I helped a friend, Sian Roberts, rewrite her résumé. Sian has a naturally lively personality but her résumé did not reflect that – it was rather bland. No wonder she didn't get many job interviews.

I spoke to her at length and it transpired that she had spent some time teaching English in Rio de Janeiro and, while there, went on a trip up the Amazon looking for crocodiles to photograph. She had also flown a light plane over the Andes in Peru (but only for about two minutes!) After some persuasion she agreed to include both items on her résumé, although she was not that keen because, as she said, 'You don't put things like that in résumés.'

Her new résumé got her a good job shortly afterwards, simply because it did what it was meant to do: it attracted attention and persuaded an employer to want to meet this remarkable-sounding woman. If you have done anything interesting or different – include it. So many interesting people send out dull résumés. Don't be one of them.

If advertisers can get away with writing copy that actively shows a product in its best light, you should do the same. If it includes showing a professional-looking photo of the product, they will. Do the same – if you look presentable! So many applicants insist on being too nice about the task in hand. Your aim is to get the result *you* want. Anything is fair game in writing job applications, so long as you don't lie outright.

Your written presentation must be immaculate: no typos or poor grammar. Both the letter and résumé should be typewritten (make sure there's new ribbon in the typewriter/on your printer). Use a high-grade 'heavier' type of paper (approximately 100 g upwards). White seems to be best but there is an argument for using a colour to help it stand out from the crowd. If you choose to use a colour, avoid anything too bright. When the recipient holds your application he or she should be able to feel the 'quality'. The envelope should also be of similarly 'heavy' paper stock.

It's a fact that the numbers of applications for good jobs are substantially lower than applications for mediocre or mundane jobs. Many people don't apply for the good jobs simply because they 'know' they won't get them.

By attracting attention to your application successfully you will be far more likely to be invited for an interview. Assuming you are asked to attend one, you will have succeeded in stage one of the job-selection process: persuading them to take you seriously for the job.

The Interview Stage two involves more persuasion if you are to be successful. Traditionally, being interviewed is regarded as a bit like being the sacrificial lamb at the slaughter – but in reality an interview can be an opportunity to manipulate the interviewer(s) into wanting you to take the job. Somehow I can sense you don't believe me!

Let's look at the situation logically. They have a need and you have been invited to satisfy that need. They are busy people who would not waste their time asking to see you if they thought you were not suitable for the post. All you have to do is show them that in choosing you, they will have made the right choice.

To get the result you want, you must understand fully what they want and then tailor what you say, how you look and behave to match it completely. Interviews are little more than performances – for both interviewee and interviewer. No professional would perform without preparation and rehearsal. An amateur certainly cannot afford to go into such a situation without adequate preparation.

When you walk into the interview, the interviewer will genuinely want to feel that in meeting you, the right candidate has been found. Most interviewers want an easy life – so make it easy for them – gently take the lead. This does not mean rushing in as 'personality of the year' – aim for quiet self-confidence. Look in control. Tell yourself that they need you more than you need them. Even though you may feel nervous inside, it's highly unlikely that the interviewer will know this.

Use the interviewer's name – if you did not catch it, ask again. You will appear more confident using his or her name and he or she will like this. Maintain eye contact; don't look nervously at the floor. When asked about yourself don't go on as if in the confessional – keep it brief, up-beat and relevant. Rehearse beforehand so you do not 'um' and 'er' too much.

In your preparation you should have found out as much as possible about the company. This can be done from newspaper cuttings, your local library and, most importantly, from the company itself. Feel free to telephone the company and speak to a few people about what they do. Large companies often have a PR department: tell them why you are calling. Ask for the names of employees they would recommend you talk to. By showing an interest you will learn a lot about what the company does, how it fits into its industry and how well it is doing.

To make a good impression you should use this information throughout the interview. But do *not* make the common mistake of blurting it all out. Use the knowledge to formulate lots of intelligent questions about the company. Have them on a piece of paper if necessary. Let the interviewer do most of the talking. This way you will succeed in a number of ways – you will appear interested and, the more you let him or her talk, the more interesting *you* will seem! You will also be turning a one-sided interview into a two-way conversation.

Controlling the interview is important – controlling how it ends is crucial. During the interview, concentrate on issues relating to your prospective employer's needs rather than just your own. Then, when you know that the interview is coming to an end, take control by asking if there is anything else the interviewer would like to know about you. If not, say thank you for the opportunity to meet with him or her and ask when you can expect to hear from the company. By gently taking charge of the meeting you will be asserting yourself and will ensure that you are not dismissed.

Using the example of getting a job has been deliberate, to show you that it is possible to exert a level of control in situations that may at first seem totally uncontrollable. The same criteria apply in so many other areas of life.

Persuasion

The final stage in achieving maximum levels of control in your life is to know how to persuade and, to a certain extent, manipulate others to help you achieve your goals and ambitions. I am not suggesting deviousness in your dealings with others, but once you have decided on your purpose in life and the goals you must meet to fulfil that purpose, it is often necessary to enlist the help of others.

To take control effectively without appearing pushy or arrogant requires an ability to understand people. Like so many of the truly important things in life we are not normally taught how to do this in our schools and colleges. Dealing with others is therefore left almost purely to chance.

The ability to persuade others is probably the single most important quality we can ever possess. Remember how precious time is: your ability to persuade others to give you some of theirs willingly is linked directly to your success potential. This book has shown how the real power belongs to those corporations and individuals who have the skill and resources to convince us to use their products and services. Millions of people never realize what they are subjected to. Now that *you* know, use this knowledge to your advantage. If you can learn to be an effective persuader you will almost certainly achieve more in your lifetime.

In his fascinating book *The Power of Persuasion*, Rupert Eales-White cites four persuasion approaches:

Logic: using structured facts or opinions.

Incentives: dangling the most appropriate 'sticks or carrots' in front of the 'persuadee(s)'.

Group: encouraging others to 'belong' when they need to share common concepts and visions.

Empathy: concentrating attention on the needs of the persuadee to create a 'win–win' situation.

How you use these persuasion techniques and in which combination will determine how successful you will be as a persuader.

In order to motivate others to do what you want they must be inspired to want to do it for themselves. This is achieved by appealing directly to their needs. Try to put yourself in their place and figure out what would make them want to do a particular job. Ask yourself what people do to make you feel good, then do those things for others.

Think again about Maslow's 'hierarchy of needs': survival, shelter, food, love, security, acceptance, respect, knowledge, fulfilment, sex and self-esteem. You will be far more likely to succeed in persuading others if you can satisfy one or more of these needs for them.

Tactless (and unsuccessful) persuaders might use threats to try to get someone to do what they want. They rely on fear, criticism, public ridicule and lecturing to 'motivate' others. A more effective persuader would offer 'persuadees' a genuine opportunity to lighten their workload or help them to appear more effective to their superiors or colleagues.

People you may be trying to persuade might be susceptible to an approach that allows them to join or stay within 'the safety' of a particular group. Others may want to be closer to those they admire – can you help them to achieve that? Can you offer them the chance to be seen to be the best? Can you appeal to their snobbishness? Will they be able to fulfil a goal or ambition if they help you?

If you don't know what those around you want, don't just guess – ask them. If at first you don't get a satisfactory answer, be persistent. Make them see that you are really interested in what they want and why they want it. I know a successful computer salesperson who literally doubled his sales commission by incorporating the following question in his sales calls: 'What can I do to make you look good in your organization?' The strong relationships he has forged this way have practically guaranteed him future business.

To persuade effectively you must develop the ability to evoke genuine enthusiasm, not only for the tasks in hand but for the people who can best perform them. The power of enthusiasm should never be underestimated. Enthusiasm alone is sometimes enough to galvanize support from others. If you also provide encouragement, honest and genuine praise, you will achieve even better results. A sincere 'thank you' will often make someone's day and motivate him or her to do even more for you next time. By showing a genuine interest in the well-being of those you work and live with, you will not only gain their respect but their ongoing co-operation.

We often need to persuade anonymous officials and public servants to help us. Dealing with them can often be an uphill struggle. But try this approach: ask for their names (making sure that they don't suspect you of planning to use it against them in future!) and then make a point of using it while you are talking to them. Our own names are the most important words we know, so making someone feel important (particularly someone who is rarely treated in this way) will often get what you want.

At all other times try to get into the habit of asking for the names of everyone you come into contact with, then try to remember them for future use. It's a personal compliment when someone is made to feel that he or she is important enough for you to bother to remember. Such behaviour will make you stand out, because most people don't listen carefully enough when introduced to others.

Being successful at persuading others requires practice and application. It means devoting your time to listening rather than doing all the talking, asking questions instead of trying to provide all the answers. By giving 'persuadees' opportunities to contribute to the tasks you have set, you will succeed in getting them more involved and therefore more interested in the outcome.

Conclusion

I have written a great deal in this book about how everyone is constantly trying to attract your attention and take a little of your time. By asking you to *press pause on your life* and read this book I have been guilty of using up some of your time. I sincerely hope that it has been time well spent, providing you with the necessary information and food for thought to enable you to exert maximum control in your life.

I have tried to present you with a realistic and thought-provoking view of these sophisticated times. As you have seen, the voluminous market research data on us all makes it very clear that what the marketers do is not in our best interests. The pursuit of profit means they will continue to treat us disrespectfully. This ill-treatment will never cease.

Hundreds of years ago power belonged to the Church; society's scholars were the monks and clergy. Because they wrote the books they effectively told everyone what to think. Times change but the basic principle remains the same: information is power. At least these days we have a choice: we can allow those with commercial and political power to manipulate us into behaving in particular ways or we can gently take back control of our own lives. They'll try to keep you too busy coping with life to question their actions. Don't let them.

Control is available to those who want it. By using a silent 'no' we can effectively filter out and eliminate a high proportion of the people, activities and pressures that would otherwise distract us from happiness, fulfilment and true success. Personal control in our lives can only happen if we learn to say 'no' more often to the many unwanted demands on our time and attention.

As I was preparing this manuscript a number of different people read it at various stages of completion. All of them made invaluable comments. A few said how some of the text was 'just common sense' – yet one person's common sense is another's useful new piece of information. My apologies for the parts you may think are 'just common sense' – I hope you will agree that sometimes even simple things need pointing out.

Every effort is made by the manipulators to provide us all with 'the easy option'; consequently millions of us are no longer involved in our own lives. We seem willing to allow others to dominate our time. I am even more convinced now than I was when I embarked on the researching and writing of this book that being in control is not only essential for success and happiness but relatively easy to achieve.

Interestingly for me, as part of my personal plan to complete this manuscript I made a decision to stop watching TV for four months. I missed favourite programmes such as *LA Law*, *MASH*, *Have I Got News for You* and a selection of movies, but as for the rest – I didn't miss much. My life slowed right down, even though I still spent a lot of my working life in the middle of one of the busiest and most exciting cities in the world.

When I consciously chose to regain maximum control in my life, I noticed a number of interesting effects.

I came to realize that when I didn't know what programmes were on TV, I couldn't miss them. Some TV colleagues ask how I can justify working in the industry without watching TV. Noel Coward has provided a perfect answer: 'Television is something you appear on: one doesn't watch it!' I also stopped filling my life reading about programmes and their stars.

Three to four hours have been saved every day just from TV, freeing up time to devote to far more work and social activities; *Getting-ahead* tasks, I have got to know my friends properly, learned all sorts of new skills, found time to appreciate where

I live – being a tourist in London is even better fun when you live there! I now take time to read many of those books which had simply looked good on my bookshelves. Personal stress has been reduced because I have learned to be realistic when planning activities.

Looking back over what I have just written, you would be forgiven for thinking such self-interest is rather selfish, but the reality is far from it.

Today's society teaches us all to be selfish; by filling it with so many time-consuming activities which purport to make us 'feel good', we crave even more experiences if and when these activities fail to live up to our expectations. Since learning to spot many of life's 'professional distractions' and then avoid them, I have found that there is far more time to devote to my family, friends and the organizations which matter to me.

In short, after all these years, finally I have become involved in my own life. I am absolutely convinced that taking control of your life will do the same for you.

There are many organizations that would prefer that much of the information included in this book was not widely known. Consequently it is possible that certain areas of the media will be less than keen on bringing this book to the attention of a wider audience. Therefore, if you have found this book particularly helpful, it could be that some of your family, friends and colleagues would also benefit from reading it. Spread the word; help others to gain control of their lives. Yes, I will also benefit financially if I 'manipulate' you into recommending this book to others (a total royalty of 30p per copy, to be precise!) If you were to recommend it to six different people, who in turn recommended it to six others each, word would soon get around. Thank you.

Now press *Play* on your life and stop reading this book!

Further Reading and Resources

Edward de Bono, *De Bono's Thinking Course* (Ariel, 1982).

J.A.C. Brown, *Techniques of Persuasion: From Propaganda to Brainwashing* (Penguin, 1983).

Dale Carnegie, *How to Develop Self-Confidence and Influence People by Public Speaking* (Cedar Books, 1945).

––, *How to Win Friends and Influence People* (Cedar Books, 1938).

Penny Chorlton, *Cover Up: Taking the Lid off the Cosmetics Industry* (Grapevine/Thorsons, 1988).

Eric Clark, *The Want Makers* (Hodder & Stoughton, 1988; Coronet Paperback, 1989).

Andrew Crofts, *Hype: The Essential Guide to Marketing Yourself* (Hutchinson Business Books, 1990).

Harvey and Marilyn Diamond, *Fit for Life* (Bantam Books, 1985).

––, *Living Health* (Warner Books, 1987).

Dr Wayne W. Dyer, *Pulling Your Own Strings* (Arrow, 1979).

Rupert Eales-White, *The Power of Persuasion* (Kogan Page, 1992).

Tom Hopkins, *The Official Guide to Success* (Panther, 1982).

William Meyers, *The Image Makers – Secrets of Successful Advertising* (Orbis, 1984).

Dr Robert Montgomery, *The Truth About Success and Motivation* (Thorsons, 1987).

Vance Packard, *The Hidden Persuaders* (Penguin, 1957).

Sogyal Rinpoche, *The Tibetan Book of Living and Dying* (Rider Books, 1992).

Anthony Robbins, *Unlimited Power* (Simon & Schuster, 1989).

Denis Waitley, *Seeds of Greatness* (World's Work, 1983).
Zig Ziglar, *See You At The Top* (Pelican, 1974).

Useful address:

> TFSR (Tools for Self-Reliance)
> Head Office
> Netley Marsh
> Southampton
> SO4 2GY
> UK

Please include a stamped self-addressed envelope.

Press Pause on Your Life . . . and Listen to These Tapes

This six-part audio cassette series features a professionally recorded condensed version of this book. The series runs for approximately four hours. The tapes are narrated by Roy Sheppard, author of this book.

To order your cassettes send a cheque or money order for £44.95 (includes p & p and VAT) to:

The Celebrity Store Ltd.
16a Crown Road
Twickenham
Middlesex TW1 3EE
UK.

Orders can only be accepted when accompanied by full payment in sterling. Please allow 28 days for delivery. Overseas orders should add £10 to cover additional postage costs.

For further details of Roy Sheppard's *Press Pause on Your Life* conferences, seminars and staff and management training courses, contact The Celebrity Store Ltd. at the address given above (Fax: 081–891 3430).

Cut out this page and display it in a prominent place at home or at work. Why not give copies to your friends?

10 Ways to Help You Control Your Life

- Just because something is available, it does not mean it is worth having.

- Constantly ask yourself 'Is this the best use of my time?'

- Are you too busy watching others living their lives to live yours to the full?

- Are you the result of what 'happens to you', or do you spend your time 'making things happen'?

- Life's 'players' have all the fun, but 'spectators' think *they* do!

- Don't put off *Getting-ahead* tasks in favour of *Catching-up* tasks.

- Develop a 'purpose' in your life; if it is strong enough you won't allow anyone to distract you from success, fulfilment and happiness.

- To persuade others, combine the following: incentives, logic, 'joining the crowd' and, above all, empathy!

- Learn to say 'No' more often without feeling bad about it.

- If you don't have a personal plan in life, you are part of somebody else's!

Taken from *Press Pause on Your Life* by Roy Sheppard, published by Thorsons (1993)

Of further interest . . .

THE PURSUIT OF HAPPINESS

Who Is Happy – And Why?

David G. Myers

We all want to be happy, but if we ask what happiness is, or what causes it, the answers are not always so easy to find. Yet, if this is such an important subject for us, why do we understand so little about it?

In this fascinating exploration of the nature and value of happiness, social psychologist David Myers investigates such questions as:

- **Can money buy happiness?**
- **Who are the happily married?**
- **Is good health linked to happiness?**
- **Why is work so important for well-being?**
- **Is happiness rare?**

Using the results of hundreds of recent studies, Myers explodes some of the popular myths about happiness which so many of us share. He then identifies those key inner traits which *do* enable it to grow and outlines a number of practical steps we can all take to discover greater peace and joy.

WANT TO CHANGE BUT I DON'T KNOW HOW

A Step-by-Step Programme for Mastering your Life

Tom Rusk and Randy Read

'I want to change my life but I don't know how. I'm stuck – I know things aren't quite right, but I'm not sure what to do.'

Stop and ask yourself whether your life is going where you want it to . . . and don't be surprised if you don't like the answer! Discovering your own path is the toughest job there is – but help is at hand. Rusk and Read's step-by-step plan will provide the maps and tools to help you find what's right for you. With practical, inspiring advice, exercises and case studies, *I Want to Change But I Don't Know How* will set you free for a new beginning:

- **acknowledge your self defeating attitudes and banish them forever**

- **listen to your inner needs and learn to love what you hear**

- **recognize your natural talents and skills**

- **learn to develop happier and healthier relationships**

- **if you want to change, you can start now!**

TAKE CHARGE OF YOUR LIFE

How Not to Be a Victim

Louis Proto

Do you ever feel:

- **trapped**
- **helpless**
- **under pressure**

If your answer is 'very often' or 'all the time' then you could well be caught in the victim trap without knowing it.

In fact no one can make us victims unless we allow them to and in *Take Charge of your Life* Louis Proto hands us the tools to get out of the victim trap before it snaps shut. He shows that more often than not we can choose our reaction to what happens to us and use our experiences to grow more whole.

This inspiring book asks questions which can unblock defences against change and then offers support through relaxation and visualization. Filling time and space for ourselves, creating more harmonious relationships, and emerging from financial and emotional pressures can all be achieved by learning how to get back the power we have given away and then using it to create the quality of life we want for ourselves.

STRESS BUSTERS

Over 100 Strategies for Stress

Robert Holden

STRESS RELIEF
STRESS RELEASE
STRESS CONTROL

Stress Busters is a creative, practical guide to successful stress control – packed with effective coping strategies for achieving positive health, personal happiness and peak performance. These include tips, tactics and techniques for:

deep relaxation • anxiety control • problem solving • creative thinking • self-esteem • good health • pain relief • better sleep • energy management • happy relationships

and a host of other stress-related issues.

Robert Holden set up the first Stress Buster Clinic on the National Health Service in Great Britain. As a successful Stress Control Consultant, he has designed Personal Empowerment Programmes for local government, the BBC, doctors, health professionals, business and industry, and for the general public. His other books include *Laughter, the Best Medicine*.

TOO PERFECT

When Being in Control Gets Out of Control

Allan Mallinger and Jeanette de Wyze

So you're a perfectionist. You pride yourself on being reliable, hard-working and self-disciplined. Your office and home are neat and organized, and you are always in control. You are successful and financially secure.

But there is a downside. You may be confident and poised on the outside, but chances are you are hurting inside. The standards you set yourself and others are so high you are constantly setting yourself up for disappointment, and your rigidity may be preventing you from enjoying life and forming healthy relationships. Other traits of the perfectionist include:

- **A fear of making errors**
- **A strong devotion to work**
- **A need for order or firm routine**
- **Frugality**
- **A need to know and follow the rules**
- **Emotional guardedness**
- **A tendency to be stubborn**
- **An inclination to worry**
- **A need to be above criticism**

Too Perfect is a compelling look inside the often painful world of the obsessive personality, offering insights and hope for those caught in its grip.

EVEN EAGLES NEED A PUSH

Learning to Soar in a Changing World

David McNally

Young eagles do not learn to fly until they are pushed out of their safe nest. Until they learn to soar, they do not discover the privilege it is to have been born an eagle.

This book is about your success, your happiness, your work and your dreams.

It is about the power to create what you want for your life.

It is about discovering a true sense of purpose, the contribution that only you can make to the world.

It is about courage, determination and commitment. And it is about love and appreciation.

Most of all, it is about rising above the turbulence of these uncertain yet exciting times to chart a meaningful course for your future.

THE STRESS PROTECTION PLAN

How to Stay Healthy under Pressure

Leon Chaitow

Do you suffer from migraine, chronic back pain, frequent colds, fatigue, panic attacks, high blood pressure? If so, too much stress could be damaging your health!

We now know that stress has a disastrous effect on our immune systems, and can be the major cause of both mild *and* serious health problems.

Psychoneuroimmunology, or PNI, is the new science which holds the key to many common health problems. It points to new ways to control these damaging emotions and so protect our bodies' natural defences and ward off illness.

Leading health writer Leon Chaitow here uses the latest research into the mind/body connection to explain how to create your own stress protection plan.

This is a system that really works, that you can tailor to each type of stressful situation, including advice on diet, exercise, meditation, relaxation, guided imagery, visualization, and checklists to assess your progress.

Don't let the inevitable pressures of life do a demolition job on your well-being. Work out your own Stress Protection Plan – before it's too late!